GUYS OVER 50:

THE DOS AND DON'TS OF DATING

STARTER EDITION

J.D. Zarate

DEDICATION

This book is dedicated to the old me. I wished older me could have told my younger self this information, it would have saved me a lot of grief.

CONTENTS

THE DOS AND DON'TS FOR SINGLE GUYS OVER 50

So, you find yourself single and near 50 or maybe over 50. Regardless of how you got here, you are here. So, what's your plan? Are you planning on staying single? Are you planning on maybe dating? Are you just going to sit on a couch and waste your time watching TV?

Why don't you take a small challenge, a challenge to become a better version of yourself, after all what do you have to lose? You can take a small challenge to improve yourself and see what happens if you take small steps to becoming a better you.

This book is not in sequence. You will read as you go and start to make improvements as you go in life. There is no "one shoe fits all" in guys, we are all uniquely different. If you read something and you need to make an improvement, make it. If you are already good in that area of your life, then move on to where you need help.

So, let's begin.

FOR STARTERS: APPEARANCE

One of the first things you want to do is improve how you look. What you need to do is take a good look in the mirror and ask yourself, would you date you? How is your appearance? Is your hair neat and cut? Are you well groomed? Do you have a cornhusk sticking out of your nose and ears?

One of the first thing women look at is your face. The whole beauty and the Beast stuff only works in the movies. For a woman to say they like you on the inside takes time. So, this is a small step we can take.

Now you want to improve what you have. This means getting a haircut and always keeping your hair nice. I know for some this might be a task. Some guys just don't like getting their haircut and I get it, but your challenge is to become a better you, so a better you will need to have nice hair. I would go out and find a good barber/stylist and commit to getting a haircut routine. This could be once a month to every two weeks, whatever helps keep your hair in check is what you need to do. Now when it comes to me, I get a haircut every two weeks. I find this keeps me looking the same way, so people are used to my look.

Now your ears. Unless your hair covers your ears, the little hairs you have there need to be groomed. This does not take much, go out and buy a small grooming razor from the store and groom those ears. Next is your nose hairs. One thing most woman don't like is a man with more nose hair than he has on his own head. I would start out once a week and groom myself. It won't take long, and soon you will get to a routine.

Now skin appearance. Take a good look at your skin. What kind of skin do you have? Is it dry? Oily? You will need to get a good men's facial cleanser and begin a washing routine for yourself. Also, it would benefit you to use wrinkle serums. Your appearance is important and removing a line or two will do you good.

Let's look at your clothes. I know everyone has their own style and I'm not here to change anything, I just want your clothes to look good. For starters, no old clothes that look worn out. No clothes with worn out holes either. Another big thing don't dress like a twenty year old, it just looks bad and women will think you're a "tool". Dress age appropriate. You should always dress as if you are meeting someone. I've seen many guys look bad because they were maybe going to the gym or maybe doing errands, I'm not saying wear a suit, just wear clothes that someone might get a good first impression of you.

Ok, this is just a start. We can try to fix what the world sees.

GUYS OVER 50
SHOULD BE IN SHAPE.

Being in shape is important for guys over 50, as it can help promote good health, prevent chronic diseases, and improve overall quality of life. Here are some tips to help guys over 50 stay in shape:

1. Exercise regularly: Regular exercise can help improve cardiovascular health, build strength and endurance, and maintain a healthy weight. Aim for at least 30 minutes of moderate intensity exercise most days of the week.

2. Strength training: Strength training can help build muscle mass and bone density, which can be particularly important for guys over 50. Aim for at least two days of strength training each week.

3. Stretching: Regular stretching can help improve flexibility, reduce the risk of injury, and relieve tension and stiffness. Consider incorporating stretching exercises into your routine several times a week.

4. Healthy eating: Eating a healthy, balanced diet that's rich in fruits, vegetables, lean proteins, and whole grains can help fuel your body and support good health.

5. Get enough sleep: Getting enough sleep is important for overall health and well-being. Aim for seven to eight hours of sleep each night.

GUYS OVER 50
SHOULD GET RID OF BAD HABITS.

Yes, it's always a good idea to get rid of bad habits to improve overall health and well-being. Here are some common bad habits that guys over 50 may need to address:

1. Smoking: Smoking is a major health hazard, and quitting smoking is one of the best things you can do for your health.

2. Excessive drinking: While moderate drinking is fine, excessive alcohol consumption can lead to a host of health problems, including liver damage and high blood pressure.

3. Poor diet: A diet high in processed foods and sugar can lead to obesity, high blood pressure, and diabetes. Eating a balanced diet of whole foods can help prevent these health issues.

4. Sedentary lifestyle: Sitting for long periods of time can lead to a host of health problems, including weight gain, high blood pressure, and increased risk of heart disease. Incorporating regular exercise into your daily routine can help prevent these issues.

5. Poor sleep habits: Not getting enough sleep or having poor quality sleep can lead to a range of health problems, including

depression, anxiety, and increased risk of heart disease. Developing good sleep habits, such as sticking to a regular sleep schedule and avoiding caffeine before bed, can help improve sleep quality.

By making positive changes to these habits, guys over 50 can improve their overall health and well-being, and become more attractive as a date.

GUYS OVER 50
SHOULD BE CENTERED.

Being centered means having a sense of inner calm and balance, and can be an attractive quality for anyone, including guys over 50. Here are some tips on how to cultivate a sense of centeredness:

1. Practice mindfulness: Mindfulness involves paying attention to the present moment with a non-judgmental attitude. This can help you become more aware of your thoughts and emotions, and develop a greater sense of inner calm.

2. Cultivate self-awareness: Being aware of your own needs, desires, and emotions can help you stay grounded and centered in your interactions with others.

3. Take care of yourself: This means getting enough sleep, eating well, and engaging in activities that bring you joy and relaxation.

4. Practice stress-reducing techniques: This could include exercise, meditation, or deep breathing exercises.

5. Set boundaries: Being able to say "no" to things that don't serve you can help you feel more centered and in control of your own life.

By cultivating a sense of centeredness, guys over 50 can project a sense of calm and stability, which can be attractive to others.

GUYS OVER 50
SHOULD NOT BE "TOOLS".

It's important for all individuals, regardless of age or gender, to treat others with respect and kindness. Being a "tool" - that is, behaving in a selfish or insensitive manner - can harm others and damage relationships.

As people age, it becomes more important to prioritize relationships and connections with others, whether that means family, friends, or romantic partners. Treating others poorly or disrespecting their feelings or needs can ultimately lead to loneliness and isolation.

Instead, it's important to cultivate positive qualities and behaviors that foster healthy, fulfilling relationships with others. This may include being empathetic, supportive, and communicative, as well as being willing to listen and learn from others.

Ultimately, being a kind and respectful person can have numerous benefits, both for your own well-being and for the well-being of those around you. By treating others with compassion and understanding, you can build strong, meaningful connections that can last a lifetime.

GUYS OVER 50
SHOULD EXALT WISDOM.

As people age, they often gain a greater degree of life experience and wisdom, which can be valuable both for their own personal growth and for the benefit of others.

Exalting wisdom means recognizing the value of this experience and using it to guide your actions and decisions. This may involve taking a more thoughtful and deliberate approach to problem-solving, seeking out new learning opportunities to continue expanding your knowledge and skills, and sharing your insights and advice with others who may benefit from your perspective.

At the same time, it's important to balance this wisdom with an open-minded and flexible approach to life. Being to set in your ways or resistant to change can limit your growth and potential, both personally and professionally.

Ultimately, the key is to cultivate a healthy balance between experience and adaptability, using your wisdom to inform your decisions while remaining open to new ideas and experiences. By embracing a growth mindset and continuing to learn and evolve over time, you can continue to thrive and make meaningful contributions to the world around you.

GUYS OVER 50 SHOULD LIVE WITH NO REGRETS.

Living life without regrets is a worthy goal for people of all ages, but it can be especially important for older guys who may be reflecting on their past experiences and looking ahead to the future.

To live with no regrets means embracing the present moment, learning from past mistakes, and striving to create a fulfilling and meaningful life going forward. This may involve taking risks, trying new things, and pursuing your passions and interests without fear of failure or judgment.

At the same time, it's important to acknowledge and learn from past mistakes and missed opportunities, rather than dwelling on them or letting them hold you back. This may involve practicing self-compassion and forgiveness, as well as taking proactive steps to address any unresolved issues or challenges from your past.

Ultimately, the key to living with no regrets is to cultivate a sense of gratitude and acceptance for the life you have lived and the person you have become. By focusing on the positive and embracing new opportunities for growth and learning, you can create a life that is rich with meaning, purpose, and fulfillment.

GUYS OVER 50 SHOULD NOT LIVE IN THE PAST.

As people age, it can be easy to get caught up in nostalgia and to long for the past, whether it's a particular time in their life or a relationship that has ended. However, dwelling on the past can ultimately prevent you from fully embracing the present and creating a fulfilling future.

Living in the past can also be a form of avoidance or denial, as it allows you to avoid dealing with the challenges and uncertainties of the present moment. Instead of facing these challenges head-on and working to create positive change, you may find yourself stuck in old patterns and routines, unable to move forward.

To avoid living in the past, it's important to cultivate a sense of mindfulness and presence in your daily life. This may involve practicing meditation or other mindfulness exercises, as well as taking time to appreciate and savor the moments of joy and connection that you experience each day.

It's also important to acknowledge and process any unresolved emotions or experiences from your past, rather than suppressing them or pushing them aside. This may involve seeking out therapy or counseling to help you work through these issues in a safe and supportive environment.

Ultimately, by embracing the present moment and working to create a positive and fulfilling future, you can break free from the limitations of the past and create a life that is full of meaning, purpose, and joy.

GUYS OVER 50
SHOULD TAKE THAT RISK.

Taking risks can be a powerful way for older guys to expand their horizons, try new things, and create a life that is rich with meaning and purpose. Whether it's starting a new business, pursuing a lifelong dream, or taking a leap of faith in a personal relationship, taking calculated risks can be an important part of personal growth and development.

Of course, it's important to weigh the potential benefits and risks of any given decision before taking action. This may involve doing your research, seeking out advice from trusted friends or professionals, and considering the potential outcomes and consequences of your actions.

At the same time, it's important to avoid getting stuck in a rut or becoming overly risk-averse, as this can prevent you from taking advantage of new opportunities and experiences. By embracing a mindset of growth and adventure, and by being willing to take calculated risks when the situation warrants it, you can create a life that is rich with excitement, challenge, and fulfillment.

Remember, taking risks doesn't always mean taking huge, life-altering leaps. Sometimes it can be as simple as trying a new hobby or activity, reaching out to make new friends, or taking a chance on a new job or career path. Whatever the situation, by embracing a spirit of openness and curiosity, and by being willing to take calculated risks when the opportunity arises, you can create a life that is full of joy, meaning, and purpose.

GUYS OVER 50 SHOULD ALWAYS BE MOTIVATED TO MOVE FORWARD NOT BACKWARDS.

As people get older, it can be easy to fall into the trap of complacency and to become comfortable with the status quo. However, staying motivated and continuing to move forward is essential for personal growth, development, and fulfillment.

One way to stay motivated is to set goals for yourself and to work toward achieving them. These goals might be related to your career, your personal relationships, your health and fitness, or any other area of your life that you feel is important. By setting specific, measurable, and achievable goals, you can create a clear roadmap for your future and work toward creating the life you want.

Another way to stay motivated is to stay engaged with the world around you. This might involve staying informed about current events, taking part in social or community activities, or pursuing hobbies and interests that keep you engaged and stimulated. By staying engaged and active, you can continue to grow and learn, and you can avoid feeling stuck or stagnant.

Of course, staying motivated isn't always easy, and there will inevitably be challenges and setbacks along the way. However, by embracing a positive attitude and by remaining focused on your goals and priorities, you can overcome these challenges and continue to move forward with confidence and purpose. Ultimately, by staying motivated and continuing to move forward, you can create a life that is rich with meaning, purpose, and joy, no matter what your age.

GUYS OVER 50
SHOULD DO THINGS THAT
BRING HAPPINESS TO THEIR LIFE.

As people get older, it can be easy to fall into a routine and to become complacent, but it's important to continue to seek out new experiences and activities that bring happiness and joy into your life.

One way to do this is to focus on your passions and interests. Whether it's a hobby you've enjoyed for years or something new you've always wanted to try, pursuing your interests can bring a sense of purpose and fulfillment to your life. It can also be a great way to meet new people and form new connections.

Another way to bring happiness into your life is to focus on relationships. This might mean spending time with family and friends, volunteering in your community, or getting involved in social groups and organizations that align with your values and interests. Building and maintaining strong relationships can bring a sense of connection and purpose to your life, and can be especially important as you get older.

Also, taking care of your physical and mental health can also play a big role in bringing happiness and fulfillment into your life. This might mean getting regular exercise, eating a healthy diet, getting enough sleep, and seeking out support when you need it.

Ultimately, finding happiness and joy in your life is a personal journey, and it's important to experiment with different activities and approaches to find what works best for you. By staying open to new experiences and focusing on the things that bring you happiness and fulfillment, you can create a life that is rich with meaning and purpose, no matter what your age.

GUYS OVER 50
SHOULD NOT LIE TO IMPRESS
PEOPLE.

That's a good point. As people get older, it can be tempting to exaggerate or stretch the truth to impress others or to make oneself seem more interesting or accomplished. However, this can be damaging both to oneself and to the relationships we have with others.

When we lie or deceive others, we create a sense of mistrust and can damage our reputation and credibility. This can lead to strained relationships with others, and can ultimately leave us feeling isolated and alone.

Moreover, lying can also have negative effects on our own self-esteem and sense of self-worth. When we feel the need to constantly impress others with our accomplishments or experiences, we may begin to feel that we are not good enough as we are, and that we need to constantly prove ourselves in order to be accepted or valued.

Instead of lying to impress others, it's important to focus on building genuine connections and relationships based on honesty and authenticity. This means being honest about our strengths and weaknesses, and being willing to share our experiences and perspectives with others in an open and genuine way. By focusing on building strong, honest relationships with others, we can create a sense of connection and community that can bring great joy and fulfillmentinto our lives.

GUYS OVER 50
SHOULD NOT SPEND
A LOT OF MONEY TO IMPRESS
WOMEN.

A very good point. The only person you should try to impress is that guy in the mirror. While it's natural to want to impress someone we're interested in, spending a lot of money to do so can often backfire, particularly if we're doing it to compensate for other areas where we feel insecure or inadequate.

Moreover, spending money on someone else can sometimes create an imbalance in the relationship, making the other person feel indebted or obligated in ways that can be uncomfortable or undesirable.

Instead of trying to impress women with material possessions or lavish gestures, it's often more effective to focus on building a strong emotional connection based on shared interests, values, and experiences. This can involve simply spending time together doing things that you both enjoy, or engaging in deep and meaningful conversations that help you get to know each other better.

By focusing on building a genuine emotional connection with someone, rather than trying to win them over with material things, you can create a relationship that is based on mutual respect and admiration, and that is much more likely to be fulfilling and rewarding in the long run.

GUYS OVER 50 SHOULD NOT SPEND MONEY THEY DON'T HAVE.

That's an important point. As people get older, it's natural to want to enjoy the fruits of their labor and to indulge in some of the luxuries that they may not have been able to afford when they were younger. However, it's important to do so within one's means and to avoid spending money that they don't have.

Spending money that they don't have can lead to a range of financial problems, including debt, bankruptcy, and financial hardship. These problems can have long-lasting effects on a person's life, and can create a great deal of stress and anxiety.

Instead of spending money they don't have, older guys should focus on making smart financial decisions that allow them to enjoy their lives while still maintaining a healthy financial balance. This may involve creating a budget, investing in long-term savings and retirement plans, and seeking out financial advice from professionals when needed.

By taking a responsible approach to their finances, older guys can enjoy their lives and pursue their interests without putting themselves at risk of financial hardship or stress. This can create a greater sense of peace of mind and financial security, which can be especially important as they move into their retirement years.

GUYS OVER 50
SHOULD BE SAVING
THEIR MONEY.

Yes, saving money is an important consideration for older guys, especially as they approach retirement. While it's natural to want to enjoy one's money and indulge in hobbies and interests, it's important to balance that with saving for the future.

As people get older, they often have a range of financial responsibilities to consider, including mortgages, car payments, and medical bills. Additionally, retirement can bring its own set of financial challenges, including the need to rely on fixed income sources such as pensions or social security.

By saving money throughout their lives, older guys can build a financial cushion that can help them weather these challenges and enjoy their retirement years more comfortably. This can involve setting up a savings plan, such as a 401k or IRA, or simply putting money aside in a savings account.

It's also important for older guys to consider their long-term financial goals and to adjust their savings plan accordingly. This may involve consulting with a financial advisor to ensure that their investments and savings strategies are aligned with their goals.

By taking a proactive approach to saving and investing, older guys can create a secure financial future for themselves and their families, and enjoy their lives with greater peace of mind.

GUYS OVER 50
SHOULD HAVE PERSPECTIVE.

Yes, having perspective is an important trait for guys over 50. With age comes experience, and experience can lead to gaining perspective on various aspects of life. People over 50 have lived through different experiences, challenges, and changes, which can give them a broader and more insightful view of the world. This perspective can be beneficial in decision-making, problem-solving, and relationships with others.

However, it's important to note that age alone does not necessarily guarantee perspective. Some individuals may have had limited life experiences, and therefore, may not have gained a significant amount of perspective. On the other hand, younger people can also have a mature and insightful perspective, depending on their experiences and personal growth.

Ultimately, having perspective is a valuable trait, regardless of age, and it can lead to greater understanding and empathy towards others, as well as a more fulfilling life.

GUYS OVER 50 SHOULD NOT BLAME OTHERS FOR THEIR MISTAKES.

That's right! Taking responsibility for one's mistakes is an essential part of personal growth and development. Blaming others for our mistakes can hinder our ability to learn from them and make positive changes in our lives. It can also damage our relationships with others, as people generally appreciate honesty and accountability.

While it's true that people over 50 should take responsibility for their mistakes, it's important to recognize that this is a valuable trait for individuals of all ages. It's a sign of maturity and demonstrates a willingness to learn from one's experiences. By acknowledging their mistakes and taking steps to rectify them, individuals can move forward in a positive direction and improve their relationships with others.

In conclusion, while age can bring wisdom and experience, taking responsibility for one's mistakes is a trait that everyone should strive to possess, regardless of age or gender. It's an essential part of personal growth and development, and it can lead to greater happiness and success in all aspects of life.

GUYS OVER 50
SHOULD KNOW WHO THEY ARE.

It is important for anyone, regardless of their age, to have a strong sense of self and identity. For guys over 50, this can mean reflecting on their life experiences, values, and beliefs to gain a deeper understanding of who they are and what is important to them. Knowing oneself is an essential part of personal growth and development, and it's something that people of all ages should strive to achieve. However, with age comes a greater awareness of one's strengths, weaknesses, values, and goals, which can help individuals to better understand themselves and their place in the world.

By the time a person reaches 50 years of age, they have likely experienced a wide range of challenges, successes, and failures. These experiences can provide valuable insights into one's personality, preferences, and priorities. Knowing oneself can help individuals make better decisions, set realistic goals, and build more meaningful relationships with others.

However, it's important to note that self-awareness is a lifelong journey that requires ongoing reflection, self-examination, and personal growth. While people over 50 may have a greater understanding of themselves than younger individuals, they should still be open to learning, growing, and evolving.

In conclusion, knowing oneself is a crucial aspect of personal growth and development, and people over 50 should strive to continue to learn and grow in this area. By doing so, they can build a more fulfilling and meaningful life and inspire others to do the same.

GUYS OVER 50
SHOULD FEEL NEEDED.

$\mathbf{F}$ eeling needed is an important aspect of a person's sense of purpose and fulfillment in life, and it is especially relevant for guys over 50 who may be transitioning into retirement or experiencing other major life changes. Here are some ways guys over 50 can feel needed:

1. Volunteer: Find a cause that you are passionate about and volunteer your time and skills to help others. Volunteering can provide a sense of purpose and fulfillment, and it can also help you make new connections and meet new people.

2. Mentor: Use your knowledge and experience to mentor younger people in your field or community. Mentoring can be a rewarding way to give back and help others succeed.

3. Help family and friends: Offer your time and support to your family and friends. Whether it's helping with a home improvement project or offering advice and guidance, being there for your loved ones can provide a sense of purpose and meaning.

4. Pursue hobbies and interests: Engage in activities that you enjoy and that give you a sense of accomplishment. Whether

it's gardening, woodworking, or playing music, pursuing your hobbies and interests can help you feel fulfilled and needed.

5. Get involved in your community: Join a community group or organization and get involved in local initiatives. Whether it's volunteering at a food bank or participating in a neighborhood watch program, getting involved in your community can provide a sense of purpose and help you feel needed.

GUYS OVER 50
SHOULD FEEL APPRECIATED.

Feeling appreciated is important at any age, but it can be especially important for guys over 50 who may be experiencing a sense of invisibility or being overlooked. Here are some ways that guys over 50 can feel appreciated:

1. Volunteer: Volunteering can be a great way to feel appreciated while also giving back to the community. Look for organizations or causes that resonate with you and get involved.

2. Seek out meaningful relationships: Surrounding yourself with people who value and appreciate you can go a long way in boosting your sense of self-worth. Seek out friends, family members, or romantic partners who appreciate your strengths and unique qualities.

3. Celebrate your accomplishments: Take time to acknowledge and celebrate your accomplishments, both big and small. Whether it's a personal milestone or a professional achievement, give yourself credit where credit is due.

4. Pursue your passions: Engaging in activities that bring you joy and fulfillment can help you feel appreciated by yourself and others. Whether it's playing music, writing, or gardening, make time for the things that make you happy.

5. Express gratitude: Expressing gratitude for the people and things in your life can help you feel more appreciated in return. Take time to thank the people who have made a positive impact on your life and express gratitude for the blessings in your life.

GUYS OVER 50
SHOULD KNOW THEIR BOUNDARIES.

Knowing your boundaries is an important aspect of maintaining a healthy and fulfilling life, especially as you get older. Here are some tips for guys over 50 on knowing their boundaries:

1. Identify your values: Take some time to reflect on your personal values, what's important to you and what you stand for. This will help you determine what your boundaries are and what you're willing to accept or not accept in different areas of your life.

2. Learn to say no: It's okay to say no when someone asks you to do something that goes against your values or makes you uncomfortable. Saying no is not a sign of weakness, but rather a sign of strength and self-respect.

3. Set realistic expectations: Be realistic about what you can and cannot do, and communicate this to others. Don't overcommit or overpromise, as this can lead to feelings of stress and burnout.

4. Practice self-care: Take care of yourself physically, mentally, and emotionally. This includes getting enough sleep, eating

healthy, engaging in regular exercise, and setting aside time for hobbies and activities that bring you joy.

5. Trust your intuition: Pay attention to your gut feelings and intuition. If something doesn't feel right, it's probably not. Trust yourself and your instincts, and don't be afraid to speak up or make changes when necessary.

GUYS OVER 50
SHOULD HAVE A QUALITY OF CERTAINTY.

Having a quality of certainty can be beneficial for guys over 50, as it can help them feel more confident in their decisions and actions. Here are some tips on how to develop a quality of certainty:

1. Know your values: Understand what is important to you and what you stand for. This will help you make decisions and take actions that align with your beliefs and values.

2. Embrace your experience: As an older guy, you likely have years of life experience that have taught you valuable lessons. Use this experience to your advantage and trust your instincts.

3. Be open to learning: While it's important to trust your experience, it's also important to remain open to learning new things. This will help you stay up to date with current trends and technologies, and may even help you discover new passions.

4. Practice self-care: Taking care of your physical and mental health can help you feel more confident and certain in your

decisions. Make sure to prioritize self-care activities such as exercise, meditation, and getting enough sleep.

5. Surround yourself with positivity: Spending time with people who support and encourage you can help you feel more certain in your abilities and decisions. Seek out relationships and environments that make you feel good about yourself.

GUYS OVER 50
SHOULD BE NON-REACTIVE.

Being non-reactive means not letting external events or other people's behavior affect your emotions and reactions. This can be a valuable skill for guys over 50, who may have experienced a range of life events that could trigger negative emotions.

Here are some tips for developing non-reactivity:

1. Practice mindfulness: Mindfulness is a technique that helps you focus on the present moment without judgment. By practicing mindfulness regularly, you can develop the ability to observe your thoughts and emotions without being consumed by them.

2. Develop emotional regulation skills: Emotional regulation skills can help you manage your emotions more effectively. This can include techniques such as deep breathing, progressive muscle relaxation, and cognitive reframing.

3. Take breaks from technology: Technology can be a major source of distraction and stress. By taking regular breaks from technology, you can reduce your exposure to negative news and social media feeds that might trigger negative emotions.

4. Develop a growth mindset: A growth mindset is the belief that you can always improve and develop new skills. By adopting a growth mindset, you can view challenges as opportunities for growth rather than sources of frustration.

5. Practice self-care: Self-care can involve a range of activities, such as exercise, healthy eating, and relaxation techniques. By taking care of yourself, you can improve your overall well-being and increase your resilience to stress.

GUYS OVER 50 SHOULD NOT FOLLOW THE TRENDS.

While it's important for guys over 50 to stay engaged with the world and open to new experiences, it's also important to be true to oneself and not feel the need to follow every trend or fad that comes along.

Trying to keep up with every new trend can be exhausting and may even feel disingenuous. It's more important to focus on one's own interests and passions, and to pursue those things that bring personal fulfillment and happiness.

It's also important to stay current and informed about changes in the world, whether they are technological, cultural, or social. Being aware of new developments and trends can help guys over 50 stays connected to the world around them and engage with new opportunities and experiences.

Ultimately, the key is to strike a balance between staying engaged with the world and staying true to oneself. Guys over 50 should be open to new experiences and opportunities, but should also feel free to pursue their own interests and passions, regardless of whether they are currently in vogue or not.

GUYS OVER 50 SHOULD NOT TRY TO BE TRENDY.

There is no one-size-fits-all answer to this question, as individual preferences and styles can vary widely. However, it's important to remember that trying too hard to be trendy or fashionable can come across as inauthentic or insincere.

Instead of focusing on the latest fashion trends or popular styles, it may be more helpful to cultivate your own unique sense of style that reflects your personality, interests, and values. This may involve experimenting with different clothing and accessories, or seeking out styles and brands that you feel comfortable and confident in.

At the same time, it's important to keep an open mind and be willing to try new things, especially if you're interested in exploring new hobbies or interests. By staying true to yourself while also being open to new experiences and ideas, you can create a style that is both authentic and appealing.

GUYS OVER 50
SHOULD HAVE INTEGRITY.

Having integrity is an important trait for everyone, including guys over 50. Integrity means being honest, transparent, and having strong moral principles. It means doing what's right even when no one is watching and standing up for what you believe in. Integrity is a fundamental aspect of one's character, and it involves being honest, ethical, and trustworthy in all areas of life. With age comes a greater understanding of the importance of integrity, as individuals have likely experienced the consequences of both positive and negative actions.

People over 50 have likely faced numerous situations that have tested their integrity, such as work-related ethical dilemmas, personal conflicts, and difficult decisions. These experiences can help individuals to develop a strong sense of integrity and to make choices that align with their values and beliefs.

Having integrity can also benefit individuals in their personal and professional relationships. People tend to trust and respect those who exhibit integrity, and this can lead to greater opportunities and success in various aspects of life.

However, it's important to note that integrity is not something that is achieved once and for all, but rather it is a continuous process of self-reflection, growth, and improvement. People over 50 should continue to prioritize integrity in their daily lives, and be willing to admit their mistakes and make amends when necessary.

In conclusion, having integrity is a crucial aspect of personal and professional success, and people over 50 should strive to exhibit integrity in all areas of their lives. By doing so, they can build strong relationships and make a positive impact on the world around them.

GUYS OVER 50
SHOULD HAVE QUIET CONFIDENCE.

Quiet confidence is an important trait for guys over 50. It's about being secure in yourself and your abilities without feeling the need to constantly prove yourself to others. Some ways to cultivate quiet confidence include:

1. Knowing your strengths and weaknesses and being comfortable with them.

2. Setting realistic goals and working towards them with determination and focus.

3. Being open to feedback and constructive criticism, but also trusting your own judgment.

4. Being honest and authentic in your interactions with others.

5. Being humble and gracious, even when you achieve success.

6. Avoiding the need for constant validation or approval from others.

7. Staying true to your values and principles, even in the face of adversity or opposition.

8. Being able to adapt to change and uncertainty without losing your sense of purpose or direction.

By cultivating quiet confidence, guys over 50 can navigate the challenges and opportunities of life with a sense of poise, strength, and inner resilience.

GUYS OVER 50
SHOULD PURSUE THEIR PASSION.

Pursuing your passions is important at any age, and it can be especially fulfilling for guys over 50 who may be approaching retirement or looking for new challenges. Here are some tips for pursuing your passions:

1. Identify your passions: Take some time to think about what you enjoy doing and what brings you happiness. Make a list of your passions and prioritize which ones you want to pursue.

2. Make time for your passions: It's important to carve out time for your passions. Schedule time in your calendar each week to work on your passion projects, whether it's a few hours on the weekend or an hour each day.

3. Take classes or workshops: Taking classes or workshops is a great way to learn new skills and meet like-minded people who share your interests. Look for classes or workshops in your area or online.

4. Connect with others: Joining clubs or organizations related to your passions can help you connect with others who share your

interests. Attend events and meetings, and participate in group activities.

5. Use technology: Technology offers a wealth of resources for pursuing your passions. Use the internet to research your interests, watch videos, and connect with others online.

6. Be open to new experiences: Don't be afraid to try new things and explore different aspects of your passions. You may discover new interests and skills along the way.

7. Set goals: Setting goals can help you stay motivated and focused on achieving your passion projects. Set realistic goals and break them down into smaller, manageable steps.

Remember, pursuing your passions is not just about achieving a specific goal, but also about enjoying the process and finding fulfillment in your hobbies and interests. Enjoy the journey and have fun!

GUYS OVER 50
SHOULD HOLD THEIR COMPOSURE.

Yes, maintaining composure is an important aspect of being a mature and confident person, especially for guys over 50. Maintaining composure in challenging situations is a valuable trait, regardless of age or gender. However, people over 50 may have had more experience with difficult situations and have developed coping mechanisms to maintain their composure in those situations.

Holding one's composure can be especially important in professional settings, where individuals may be called upon to lead or manage others in high-pressure situations. It can also be important in personal relationships, where individuals may need to remain calm and level-headed during conflicts or disagreements.

Maintaining composure can also be beneficial to one's physical and mental health. People who are able to stay calm and manage their emotions during stressful situations are less likely to experience the negative effects of stress, such as high blood pressure, anxiety, and depression.

However, it's important to note that maintaining composure does not mean suppressing one's emotions or ignoring important issues. It's important to acknowledge and address one's emotions in a healthy way, while still maintaining a sense of composure and control.

In conclusion, holding one's composure is a valuable trait that can lead to greater success and well-being in both personal and professional settings. People over 50 may have more experience with difficult situations, but individuals of all ages can benefit from developing strategies to maintain their composure in challenging situations.

GUYS OVER 50
SHOULD BE CONFIDENT
IN THEIR AGE.

Yes, it's important for guys over 50 to be confident in their age. As they get older, they may face age-related challenges, such as changes in physical appearance, health issues, and stereotypes associated with aging. However, it's essential to embrace their age and feel confident in their experiences and wisdom they've gained over the years.

Confidence is an important trait that can help individuals to succeed and thrive in all areas of life. However, as people age, they may face societal pressures to conform to certain standards or to feel insecure about their changing physical appearance.

Being confident in one's age can be a powerful tool for personal growth and development. People over 50 have likely accumulated a wealth of life experiences and wisdom, and this can be a source of confidence and pride. They may also have a clearer sense of their values and priorities, which can help them to make better decisions and lead a more fulfilling life.

Additionally, being confident in one's age can be a positive influence on others, particularly younger generations. By embracing their age and showing pride in their life experiences, people over 50 can inspire others to do the same and to appreciate the value of aging.

However, it's important to note that being confident in one's age does not mean ignoring or denying the challenges that come with aging. It's important to address and adapt to these challenges in a healthy way, while still maintaining a positive attitude and sense of self-worth.

In conclusion, being confident in one's age can be a powerful tool for personal growth and development, and it can also inspire and influence others. People over 50 should embrace their life experiences and wisdom, while also acknowledging and addressing the challenges that come with aging.

GUYS OVER 50

SHOULD HAVE AN AUTHORITATIVE PRESENCE ABOUT THEM.

While it's important for guys over 50 to be confident and have a strong sense of self, it's also important to balance this with humility and a willingness to listen to others. Instead of focusing solely on projecting an authoritative presence, older guys should aim to be respectful, empathetic, and approachable. An authoritative presence can be an important trait for people in leadership positions or those who need to command respect and attention. As people age, they may have more experience and knowledge that can contribute to their authoritative presence.

An authoritative presence can come from a variety of factors, such as confidence, assertiveness, and a clear sense of purpose. People over 50 may have had more time to develop these traits, and may have had more experience in situations that require an authoritative presence, such as in the workplace or in public speaking.

Having an authoritative presence can also help individuals to establish boundaries and make decisions that are in their best interests. It can help to convey a sense of confidence and trustworthiness, which can be valuable in both personal and professional relationships.

However, it's important to note that an authoritative presence should not be confused with being authoritarian or controlling. It's important to balance an authoritative presence with empathy and the ability to listen to others and take their perspectives into account.

In conclusion, having an authoritative presence can be a valuable trait for people over 50, particularly in leadership or public-facing roles. However, it's important to balance this trait with empathy and the ability to listen to others, in order to establish trust and build strong relationships.

GUYS OVER 50 SHOULD NOT BE ASHAMED OF THEIR AGE.

Age is just a number, and being comfortable and confident in your own skin is attractive to others. Embrace your age and the life experience that comes with it. Don't try to hide or deny your age, but instead, use it to your advantage. Being proud of your age and who you are can make you more attractive and appealing to others. Remember, confidence is key!

Ageism is a form of discrimination that is prevalent in society, and it can lead to feelings of shame or embarrassment about getting older. However, aging is a natural part of life, and people over 50 should not be ashamed of their age.

In fact, people over 50 may have a lot to be proud of. They may have achieved personal and professional goals, gained valuable life experience and wisdom, and contributed to society in meaningful ways.

Being proud of one's age can also be a positive influence on others. It can help to challenge negative stereotypes about aging and encourage others to value the contributions of older individuals.

However, it's important to acknowledge that aging can come with its own set of challenges, such as health issues or changes in physical appearance. It's important to address these challenges in a healthy way, and to seek out support and resources when needed.

In conclusion, people over 50 should not be ashamed of their age, and should instead embrace the opportunities and experiences that come with getting older. Being proud of one's age can challenge ageist stereotypes and be a positive influence on others.

GUYS OVER 50
SHOULD BE EMOTIONALLY STABLE.

Being emotionally stable is important for anyone, regardless of age or gender. Here are some tips for guys over 50 to maintain emotional stability:

1. Practice self-awareness: Take the time to understand your emotions and how they affect your thoughts and actions. Recognize your triggers and learn to manage your emotions in a healthy way.

2. Practice stress management techniques: Stress can contribute to emotional instability, so find ways to manage your stress levels. This could include exercise, meditation, breathing techniques, or spending time in nature.

3. Seek support: Talk to trusted friends or family members about your emotions or seek the help of a therapist or counselor if needed.

4. Practice mindfulness: Stay present in the moment and focus on what's happening around you. Mindfulness can help you to manage stress and improve your emotional stability.

5. Practice gratitude: Cultivate a sense of gratitude for the positive things in your life. This can help to shift your focus away from negative emotions and improve your emotional well-being.

Ok from the head up we are starting to make progress, now from the neck down. What kind of shape are you? No shape? Some shape? Out of shape?

GUYS OVER 50
SHOULD BE DEPENDABLE.

Yes, being dependable is important for guys over 50. As they get older, they may find themselves in situations where they need to rely on others, such as in a relationship or in a job. Being dependable means being reliable and trustworthy, following through on commitments and being there when needed. It can also mean being a good listener and offering support to others. By being dependable, guys over 50 can build trust and respect with others, and ultimately enhance their relationships and life experiences.

Dependability is an important trait in personal and professional relationships. It refers to the ability to follow through on commitments and be reliable and trustworthy.

As people age, they may have more experience and a better understanding of the importance of dependability. They may have had more time to build relationships and establish a reputation for being dependable.

Being dependable can help to build trust and respect in relationships, and can also be important in achieving personal and professional goals. Dependable individuals are more likely to be given opportunities and responsibilities, and may be seen as valuable members of teams and communities.

However, it's important to note that being dependable does not mean being inflexible or unwilling to adapt to changing circumstances. It's important to communicate effectively with others and be open to feedback, in order to ensure that commitments can be met in a way that is realistic and effective.

In conclusion, being dependable is an important trait that can help to build trust and respect in personal and professional relationships. People over 50 may have had more time to build a reputation for dependability, but it's important to remain open to feedback and adaptable in order to maintain this trait.

GUYS OVER 50
SHOULD BE CENTERED.

Being centered means having a sense of inner calm and balance, and can be an attractive quality for anyone, including guys over 50. Here are some tips on how to cultivate a sense of centeredness:

1. Practice mindfulness: Mindfulness involves paying attention to the present moment with a non-judgmental attitude. This can help you become more aware of your thoughts and emotions, and develop a greater sense of inner calm.

2. Cultivate self-awareness: Being aware of your own needs, desires, and emotions can help you stay grounded and centered in your interactions with others.

3. Take care of yourself: This means getting enough sleep, eating well, and engaging in activities that bring you joy and relaxation.

4. Practice stress-reducing techniques: This could include exercise, meditation, or deep breathing exercises.

5. Set boundaries: Being able to say "no" to things that don't serve you can help you feel more centered and in control of your own life.

By cultivating a sense of centeredness, guys over 50 can project a sense of calm and stability, which can be attractive to others.

GUYS OVER 50
SHOULD KNOW THEIR WORTH.

Yes, it's important for guys over 50 to know their worth. This means recognizing their own value, strengths, and accomplishments, and not settling for less than they deserve in any aspect of their life, whether it be in relationships, career, or personal growth. It also means having healthy self-esteem and confidence in oneself, while also being open to learning and growth. Knowing one's worth can help with making better decisions, setting boundaries, and building fulfilling relationships.

Knowing one's worth is an important aspect of self-confidence and self-esteem. It involves recognizing one's skills, accomplishments, and value as a person.

As people age, they may have had more time to develop skills, gain experience, and achieve personal and professional goals. They may have a better understanding of their strengths and weaknesses, and a clearer sense of their own value.

Knowing one's worth can be important in a variety of contexts. It can help to establish boundaries in relationships, negotiate fair compensation in the workplace, and make decisions that are in one's best interests.

However, it's important to recognize that one's worth is not solely determined by external factors such as achievements or job titles. It's also important to value oneself for who they are as a person, regardless of their accomplishments or status.

In conclusion, knowing one's worth is an important aspect of self-confidence and self-esteem. People over 50 may have had more time to develop a sense of their own worth, but it's important to recognize that worth is not solely determined by external factors and to value oneself for who they are as a person.

GUYS OVER 50
SHOULD NOT BE "BAD BOYS".

I do not encourage or endorse any type of behavior that could potentially harm individuals or society. Instead, I suggest that guys over 50 should strive to be respectful, kind, and considerate towards others.

The term "bad boy" typically refers to someone who is rebellious, non-conformist, and often engages in risky or dangerous behavior. While this type of behavior may be more commonly associated with younger individuals, people of any age can exhibit these traits.

Engaging in reckless or harmful behavior can have negative consequences for oneself and others. As people age, they may have a better understanding of the potential consequences of their actions and the impact they can have on others. It's important to make responsible choices and consider the well-being of oneself and others.

Additionally, the idea of being a "bad boy" can be problematic in that it can perpetuate harmful stereotypes about masculinity and reinforce negative gender norms. Men over 50 should be encouraged to reject harmful stereotypes and instead embrace positive qualities such as empathy, compassion, and respect for others.

In conclusion, it's important for people of any age to make responsible choices and consider the well-being of themselves and others. The idea of being a "bad boy" can perpetuate harmful stereotypes and should be rejected in favor of positive qualities such as empathy and respect.

GUYS OVER 50
SHOULD NOT BE THRILL SEEKERS.

While there is nothing inherently wrong with seeking adventure or new experiences, guys over 50 should prioritize their safety and well-being. As we age, our bodies become less resilient, and it's important to take care of ourselves to prevent injuries or other health problems.

While it's important for individuals to have hobbies and activities that they enjoy, engaging in risky or dangerous behaviors solely for the purpose of seeking thrills can be problematic. As people age, they may have a better understanding of the potential consequences of their actions and the impact they can have on themselves and others.

Additionally, physical abilities and reaction times may decline as people age, which can increase the risk of injury or harm from engaging in risky activities. It's important to consider one's own physical limitations and make responsible choices accordingly.

Instead of seeking out thrills through risky behavior, men over 50 may benefit from exploring new hobbies and activities that align with their interests and abilities. This can help to promote a healthy and fulfilling lifestyle while also minimizing the potential for harm.

In conclusion, while it's important for individuals to engage in activities they enjoy, engaging in risky behavior solely for the purpose of seeking thrills can be problematic, especially as people age. Men over 50 may benefit from exploring new hobbies and activities that align with their interests and abilities instead.

GUYS OVER 50
SHOULD LOVE THEMSELVES.

Yes, self-love and self-care are important for everyone, including guys over 50. It's important to prioritize your physical and mental health, practice self-compassion, and engage in activities that bring you joy and fulfillment. When you love and care for yourself, you are better able to show up as your best self in all aspects of your life, including in relationships.

Self-love and self-acceptance are important aspects of mental and emotional well-being. They involve recognizing and valuing oneself for who they are, including their strengths and weaknesses, and treating oneself with compassion and kindness.

As people age, they may have had more time to develop a sense of self and a greater understanding of their own values and priorities. However, they may also face new challenges and transitions that can impact their self-esteem and confidence.

It's important for men over 50 to practice self-care and prioritize their own needs and well-being. This can involve engaging in activities that promote physical and mental health, setting boundaries in relationships, and seeking out support when needed.

In addition, it's important to recognize that self-love and self-acceptance are ongoing processes that require practice and effort. Men over 50 may benefit from working with a therapist or coach to develop skills and strategies for cultivating self-love and self-acceptance.

In conclusion, self-love and self-acceptance are important aspects of mental and emotional well-being, and men over 50 can benefit from prioritizing their own needs and seeking out support when needed.

GUYS OVER 50 SHOULD LEARN FROM THEIR EXPERIENCES.

Yes, learning from experiences is a valuable trait for anyone, including guys over 50. Life is full of ups and downs, and every experience we have is an opportunity to learn and grow. By reflecting on their experiences, guys over 50 can gain insights and wisdom that can help them navigate future challenges and make better decisions. It's important to be open to learning and not repeat the same mistakes, but also to recognize and appreciate the good things that have happened in their lives.

Experience is a valuable teacher, and as people age, they often accumulate a wealth of experiences that can provide valuable insights and lessons. Learning from past experiences can help individuals to make better decisions, avoid repeating mistakes, and grow and develop as individuals.

However, simply having experiences does not guarantee that one will learn from them. It's important for men over 50 to reflect on their experiences, identify key lessons learned, and apply those lessons to future situations.

Reflection can involve asking oneself questions such as:

- What did I learn from this experience?

- What worked well and what didn't?

- What could I have done differently?

- What insights can I apply to future situations?

Additionally, it's important to be open to feedback and perspectives from others, as they may have valuable insights and perspectives that can help to deepen one's understanding of past experiences.

In conclusion, learning from past experiences can help men over 50 to make better decisions, avoid repeating mistakes, and grow and develop as individuals. Reflection, openness to feedback, and a willingness to apply insights to future situations can help to facilitate this learning process.

GUYS OVER 50

SHOULD BECOME THE BEST VERSION OF THEMSELVES.

Absolutely! Age should not be a barrier to personal growth and development. In fact, as we get older, we have a wealth of life experiences and knowledge that can help us become the best version of ourselves. This can involve setting personal goals, learning new skills, trying new things, and developing a positive mindset. It's never too late to improve oneself and live a fulfilling life.

Becoming the best version of oneself involves a process of personal growth and self-improvement. It can involve setting goals, identifying areas for improvement, and taking steps to make positive changes.

For men over 50, this process can involve reflecting on their life experiences, identifying their values and priorities, and setting goals that align with these values and priorities.

Personal growth can involve developing new skills or interests, improving relationships with loved ones, enhancing physical or mental health, or pursuing new career opportunities.

However, it's important to recognize that personal growth is an ongoing process that requires commitment, effort, and a willingness to learn and change. Men over 50 may benefit from seeking out support and resources, such as therapy or coaching, to help them navigate this process and overcome any obstacles they may encounter.

In conclusion, becoming the best version of oneself is a process of personal growth and self-improvement that can involve setting goals, identifying areas for improvement, and taking steps to make positive changes. Men over 50 can benefit from reflecting on their life experiences and priorities, seeking out support and resources, and committing to ongoing personal growth.

GUYS OVER 50
SHOULD BE STRIVING FOR
LONGEVITY.

Yes, striving for longevity can be an important goal for guys over 50.

Longevity refers to living a long and healthy life, and it's something that many people strive for as they age. There are many factors that can contribute to longevity, including diet, exercise, stress management, and social support.

For men over 50, maintaining good physical and mental health can be particularly important for promoting longevity. This can involve engaging in regular exercise, eating a healthy diet, getting enough sleep, managing stress, and avoiding unhealthy habits such as smoking or excessive alcohol consumption.

In addition, maintaining social connections and a sense of purpose can also be important for promoting longevity. This can involve participating in social activities, volunteering, or pursuing hobbies or interests that provide a sense of fulfillment and purpose.

It's also important to recognize that some factors that contribute to longevity may be outside of one's control, such as genetics or environmental factors. However, by focusing on factors that are within their control, men over 50 can increase their chances of living a long and healthy life.

In conclusion, striving for longevity can involve maintaining good physical and mental health, social connections, and a sense of purpose. Men over 50 can benefit from prioritizing these factors and making positive lifestyle choices to increase their chances of living a long and healthy life.

GUYS OVER 50
SHOULD NOT TRY TO ACT YOUNGER.

That's a good point. While it's important to stay active and take care of your health, trying to act younger can come across as inauthentic and may not be attractive to others. It's important to embrace and be proud of your age and experience, rather than trying to hide or downplay it. Confidence and authenticity are attractive qualities at any age. It's important to remember that age is just a number, and there is no one "right" way to act or behave at any age. However, trying too hard to act young or keep up with younger generations can come across as inauthentic or even desperate.

Instead of trying to act a certain way based on your age, it may be more helpful to focus on cultivating positive qualities and behaviors that are timeless and ageless. This may include being kind, compassionate, and respectful to others, staying active and engaged in your hobbies and interests, and staying curious and open-minded.

At the same time, it's important to recognize and embrace the changes and challenges that come with aging, and to find ways to adapt and thrive in your current stage of life. This may involve seeking out new experiences and relationships, learning new skills or hobbies, or finding new ways to stay healthy and active.

Ultimately, the key is to be true to yourself and to focus on cultivating positive qualities and behaviors that are authentic and sustainable, rather than trying to fit into a certain mold or stereotype based on your age.

GUYS OVER 50
SHOULD HAVE PERSPECTIVE.

Yes, having perspective is an important trait for guys over 50.

Having perspective can be an important trait for men over 50. Perspective involves having a broad and balanced view of situations and events, and being able to consider different viewpoints and possibilities.

For men over 50, having perspective can involve reflecting on their life experiences and learning from them. It can also involve developing a deeper understanding of themselves and their values, and using this understanding to make decisions and navigate challenging situations.

Having perspective can also be beneficial in relationships, as it allows men over 50 to understand and empathize with the perspectives of others. This can help to build stronger and more fulfilling relationships with family, friends, and colleagues.

In addition, having perspective can be helpful in navigating transitions and changes that often occur later in life. This can involve being able to adapt to new circumstances and make adjustments as needed, while still maintaining a sense of balance and perspective.

GUYS OVER 50 SHOULD OWN THEIR MISTAKES.

Yes, owning your mistakes is an important trait at any age, but especially for guys over 50. It shows maturity, responsibility, and a willingness to learn and improve. Instead of making excuses or blaming others, owning your mistakes means taking responsibility for your actions, apologizing if necessary, and making amends if possible.

For men over 50, owning their mistakes can involve acknowledging when they have made a mistake and taking steps to make amends or correct the situation. It can also involve being open to feedback and criticism, and using this feedback to learn and grow.

Owning one's mistakes can be particularly important in relationships, as it helps to build trust and accountability. When men over 50 take responsibility for their actions, it can help to improve communication and strengthen relationships with family, friends, and colleagues.

In addition, owning one's mistakes can also be beneficial for personal growth and development. By acknowledging and learning from mistakes, men over 50 can gain valuable insights and develop greater self-awareness, which can help them to make better decisions in the future.

Overall, owning one's mistakes can be an important trait for men over 50, as it promotes accountability, improves relationships, and fosters personal growth and development.

It can also help build trust and respect in your relationships, both personal and professional.

GUYS OVER 50 SHOULD NOT BLAME OTHERS FOR THEIR MISTAKES.

That's right! Taking responsibility for your actions is an important part of personal growth and maturity, regardless of your age. It's important to recognize and learn from your mistakes instead of trying to shift the blame onto others. This can help build trust and respect in your personal and professional relationships.

Blaming others for one's mistakes can be a negative and counterproductive trait, especially for men over 50. It can create conflict and erode trust in relationships, and it can also prevent personal growth and development.

For men over 50, taking responsibility for their actions and owning their mistakes can be an important aspect of personal growth and development. It can involve acknowledging when they have made a mistake, taking accountability for the consequences, and working to make amends or correct the situation.

Blaming others for one's mistakes can also be damaging to relationships. It can create a sense of defensiveness and mistrust, and can prevent effective communication and problem-solving. By taking ownership of their mistakes and working to address them, men over 50 can build stronger and more trusting relationships with family, friends, and colleagues.

In addition, blaming others for one's mistakes can also be a sign of a lack of personal responsibility and self-awareness. By avoiding responsibility for one's actions, men over 50 may miss opportunities for personal growth and development, and may be more likely to repeat similar mistakes in the future.

Overall, avoiding the tendency to blame others for one's mistakes can be an important trait for men over 50. By taking ownership of their actions and working to address mistakes, they can promote personal growth, improve relationships, and foster a greater sense of accountability and responsibility.

GUYS OVER 50 SHOULD BE PROUD OF THEIR ACCOMPLISHMENTS.

Yes, it's important for guys over 50 to be proud of their accomplishments. As people age, they often reflect on their lives and may feel like they have not achieved as much as they wanted to. However, it's important to recognize and celebrate the things they have accomplished, no matter how small or big they may be. It can give them a sense of pride and purpose, which can contribute to their overall well-being and confidence. Additionally, being proud of their accomplishments can be attractive to others, including potential romantic partners.

Being proud of one's accomplishments can be an important trait for men over 50. It involves recognizing and celebrating one's achievements, and taking pride in the hard work and effort that went into reaching those accomplishments.

For men over 50, being proud of their accomplishments can be a way to celebrate their past successes and use them as motivation for future endeavors. It can also be a way to boost self-confidence and promote a positive self-image.

Pride in accomplishments can also be beneficial in relationships, as it can help to build respect and admiration from others. When men over 50 take pride in their accomplishments, it can inspire others and promote a sense of shared achievement and success.

In addition, being proud of one's accomplishments can also be an important aspect of overall well-being and life satisfaction. When men over 50 reflect on their past accomplishments and take pride in their successes, it can help to promote a sense of purpose and fulfillment in life.

Overall, being proud of one's accomplishments can be an important trait for men over 50, as it can promote self-confidence, build respect in relationships, and promote overall well-being and life satisfaction.

GUYS OVER 50
SHOULD EMBRACE THEIR EXPERIENCES.

Absolutely! Experiences are what shape us into the people we are today, and there's no reason to feel ashamed or embarrassed about them. Embracing one's experiences can be an important trait for men over 50. It involves recognizing the value and lessons that can be gained from past experiences, both positive and negative, and using them as a source of growth and development.

For men over 50, embracing their experiences can be a way to reflect on their past and gain a greater sense of self-awareness. By acknowledging past successes and challenges, men over 50 can identify patterns and behaviors that have helped or hindered their personal growth and development.

Embracing experiences can also be beneficial in relationships, as it can help to build empathy and understanding. When men over 50 embrace their experiences, they can relate better to others who may be going through similar challenges or experiences.

In addition, embracing experiences can also be a way to promote personal growth and development. By recognizing the lessons that can be learned from past experiences, men over 50 can use those lessons to make better decisions and navigate future challenges with greater wisdom and insight.

Overall, embracing experiences can be an important trait for men over 50, as it can promote self-awareness, build empathy in relationships, and promote personal growth and development.

GUYS OVER 50 SHOULD DO THE THINGS THEY COULD NOT DO EARLIER IN LIFE.

It's never too late for guys over 50 to try new things and pursue their passions. This could include traveling, trying new hobbies, learning new skills, or even starting a new career. It's important to remember that age is just a number and it's never too late to start something new. Don't let fear or self-doubt hold you back from exploring new opportunities and making the most out of your life.

For some men over 50, doing the things they could not do earlier in life can be a fulfilling and empowering experience. This can involve pursuing new hobbies or interests, traveling to new places, or taking on new challenges that were not possible earlier in life due to responsibilities such as work or family obligations.

Doing the things they could not do earlier in life can also be a way for men over 50 to broaden their horizons, expand their perspectives, and continue to learn and grow as individuals. It can also promote a sense of excitement and adventure, which can be invigorating and uplifting.

However, it is important for men over 50 to approach this mindset with caution and balance. While it can be empowering to pursue new experiences, it is also important to take into account personal limitations and responsibilities. It is important to make sure that pursuing new experiences does not neglect important priorities such as health, financial stability, and relationships.

In summary, for men over 50, doing the things they could not do earlier in life can be a positive and fulfilling experience. It can promote personal growth and excitement, but it is important to approach this mindset with caution and balance to ensure overall well-being and success.

GUYS OVER 50 SHOULD HAVE UNSTOPPABLE CONFIDENCE.

While having confidence is important, it's important to recognize that there may be times when even the most confident person may face setbacks or challenges. Rather than aiming for "unstoppable" confidence, it may be more helpful for guys over 50 to work on cultivating a sense of inner confidence that is grounded in their self-worth and values. This can involve focusing on their strengths, accepting their weaknesses, and being kind to themselves in the face of mistakes or setbacks. It may also involve seeking out experiences that allow them to feel successful or accomplished, such as trying a new hobby or pursuing a passion project. Ultimately, the goal is to develop a sense of confidence that is resilient and adaptable, and that allows them to navigate the ups and downs of dating and life with grace and ease.

Confidence can be an important trait for men over 50, as it can help them to navigate new challenges and experiences with greater ease and success. Unstoppable confidence can involve having a strong sense of self-worth, self-belief, and the ability to take risks and overcome obstacles.

To develop unstoppable confidence, men over 50 can start by focusing on their strengths and achievements, rather than dwelling on perceived weaknesses or failures. They can also work on developing a positive mindset, embracing challenges as opportunities for growth and learning, and setting achievable goals that align with their personal values and interests.

Practicing self-care and maintaining physical and mental health can also play a key role in developing unstoppable confidence. By prioritizing their well-being, men over 50 can feel more energized, focused, and ready to take on new challenges with greater confidence.

It is important to note, however, that developing unstoppable confidence is not about being invincible or immune to setbacks. Men over 50 may still face challenges or experience failures, but with unstoppable confidence, they can use those experiences as learning opportunities and continue to move forward with determination and resilience.

In summary, having unstoppable confidence can be an important trait for men over 50, as it can help them to navigate new challenges and experiences with greater success. By focusing on their strengths, developing a positive mindset, practicing self-care, and maintaining resilience in the face of setbacks, men over 50 can cultivate the confidence needed to pursue their goals and live their best lives.

GUYS OVER 50 SHOULD HAVE AN ABUNDANCE ATTITUDE.

An abundance attitude refers to a mindset that focuses on opportunities and possibilities rather than limitations and scarcity. It involves recognizing and appreciating what you have, rather than focusing on what you lack. It can lead to a more positive outlook on life and help individuals achieve their goals.

For people over 50, an abundance attitude can be particularly beneficial as they may be facing new challenges such as retirement, changes in health, or the loss of loved ones. By focusing on abundance, they can approach these challenges with a sense of optimism and resilience.

Overall, having an abundance attitude is a positive mindset that can benefit anyone, regardless of their age or gender.

GUYS OVER 50 SHOULD NOT OBSESS OVER A WOMAN.

When a person obsesses over another individual, it can lead to several negative consequences, such as:

1. Neglecting other important areas of their life, such as work or personal relationships.

2. Neglecting their own needs and wellbeing in favor of the person they are obsessing over.

3. Engaging in inappropriate or unhealthy behavior towards the person they are obsessing over, such as stalking or harassment.

4. Feeling anxious, depressed, or hopeless if their advances or affections are not reciprocated.

It's important for individuals to maintain a healthy perspective on relationships and to prioritize their own wellbeing. While it's natural to have feelings for someone, it's important to recognize when those feelings are becoming obsessive and to take steps to address them. This may involve seeking support from friends or a mental health professional.

GUYS OVER 50
SHOULD NOT BE A PUSHOVER.

Being a pushover means allowing others to take advantage of you or manipulate you into doing things you don't want to do. It can lead to feelings of resentment, low self-esteem, and dissatisfaction in your relationships.

It's important to set healthy boundaries in your relationships and to stand up for yourself when necessary. This doesn't mean being aggressive or confrontational, but rather being assertive and communicating your needs and boundaries in a clear and respectful manner.

As people get older, they may have more life experience and confidence to assert themselves and stand up for their own needs and values. It's important to maintain a healthy balance of assertiveness and empathy in your relationships, and to communicate openly and honestly with others.

GUYS OVER 50 SHOULD REALIZE THEY ARE SPECIAL.

Each person is special and has their own unique strengths, talents, and qualities that make them valuable and important. It's important to acknowledge and appreciate these qualities in yourself, and to recognize that you have something unique to offer to the world.

As people get older, they may have more life experience and wisdom that they can use to contribute to their communities and to help others. It's important to recognize the value of this experience and to use it to make a positive impact in the world.

Ultimately, it's important for everyone to recognize their own worth and to treat themselves with kindness, compassion, and respect. By doing so, they can lead a more fulfilling and meaningful life, and positively impact those around them.

GUYS OVER 50 SHOULD NOT HAVE A SCARCITY MINDSET WHEN IT COMES TO WOMEN.

Ascarcity mindset refers to a belief that there are limited resources or opportunities available, leading to a fear of missing out or a sense of competition with others. When applied to relationships, a scarcity mindset can lead to feelings of desperation or neediness, which can be unattractive to potential partners.

It's important to approach relationships with a mindset of abundance, focusing on the abundance of opportunities and possibilities rather than scarcity. This means recognizing that there are many potential partners out there, and that a healthy and fulfilling relationship is possible with the right person.

It's also important to maintain a healthy sense of self-worth and to avoid seeking validation or self-esteem from external sources, such as a relationship. By valuing yourself and your own needs, you can attract partners who are healthy and compatible with you.

GUYS OVER 50
SHOULD NOT BE NEEDY.

Being needy can be a sign of insecurity or low self-esteem, and can put pressure on the other person to constantly provide reassurance or attention. This can be draining and unattractive, and can ultimately lead to the deterioration of the relationship.

It's important to maintain a healthy level of independence and self-sufficiency in your relationships, while also being willing to communicate your needs and desires. This means being comfortable spending time alone, pursuing your own interests and hobbies, and having a strong sense of self-worth that isn't dependent on external validation.

At the same time, it's important to recognize that everyone has their own needs and desires in a relationship, and to communicate these needs in a clear and respectful manner. By finding a healthy balance between independence and interdependence, you can build strong and fulfilling relationships that are based on mutual respect and trust.

GUYS OVER 50
SHOULD ALWAYS BE GROWING
AND IMPROVING.

I agree that personal growth and self-improvement are important at any age, including for guys over 50. Continuing to learn and grow can lead to a more fulfilling and satisfying life, both personally and professionally.

Continuous personal growth and self-improvement can be valuable pursuits for men over 50, as they can help to promote a sense of purpose, fulfillment, and satisfaction in life. There are several ways that men over 50 can work on growing and improving themselves:

1. Learning: Men over 50 can continue to expand their knowledge and skills by taking courses, attending seminars or conferences, or simply reading books or articles on topics of interest. This can help them stay current in their fields, as well as explore new areas of interest.

2. Physical health: Men over 50 can also focus on improving their physical health by adopting healthy habits, such as regular exercise, a balanced diet, and getting enough sleep. This can help them maintain energy, vitality, and overall well-being.

3. Mental health: Men over 50 can also pricritize their mental health by practicing stress-reducing activities, such as meditation, yoga, or therapy. This can help them manage any emotional or psychological challenges that arise as they age.

4. Relationships: Men over 50 can also work on improving their relationships with loved ones, by prioritizing quality time and effective communication. Building strong, supportive relationships can help promote a sense of purpose and connectedness.

5. Giving back: Finally, men over 50 can also focus on giving back to their communities, whether through volunteering or mentorship. This can help promote a sense of purpose and fulfillment, as well as contribute to the greater good.

In summary, men over 50 can continue to grow and improve themselves in a variety of ways, from learning and maintaining physical and mental health, to improving relationships and giving back to their communities. By pursuing personal growth and self-improvement, men over 50 can live more fulfilling and satisfying lives.

GUYS OVER 50 SHOULD HAVE A PURPOSE.

I agree that having a sense of purpose is important for guys over 50 (and people of all ages) to lead a fulfilling and meaningful life. Having a clear sense of purpose can give direction and focus to your life, and provide a sense of fulfillment and satisfaction.

Purpose can come in many forms, such as pursuing a passion, volunteering for a cause you care about, or striving to make a positive impact in your community or the world. It's important to take the time to reflect on what is most important to you and what gives your life meaning and purpose, and to take steps to align your actions and goals with that purpose.

Having a sense of purpose can also be beneficial for your physical and mental health. Studies have shown that people who have a strong sense of purpose tend to be more resilient and have better mental health outcomes, and may also have a reduced risk of certain health problems.

If you're feeling uncertain about your sense of purpose, it can be helpful to engage in self-reflection and explore new opportunities or interests that align with your values and passions. By actively pursuing purpose and meaning in your life, you can lead a more fulfilling and satisfying life.

GUYS OVER 50
SHOULD HAVE PASSION.

I agree that having passion is important for guys over 50 (and people of all ages) to lead a fulfilling and satisfying life. Passion is an intense emotion that is typically associated with enthusiasm, excitement, and a strong desire to pursue a particular interest or activity.

Passion can come in many forms, such as pursuing a hobby or interest, engaging in creative pursuits, or working towards a goal or dream. Having a strong sense of passion can help you stay motivated and focused, and provide a sense of purpose and fulfillment.

One of the benefits of having passion is that it can help you maintain a positive outlook and approach to life. Pursuing activities that you are passionate about can give you a sense of joy and satisfaction, and may also help you cope with stress and difficult situations.

If you're not sure what your passion is, it can be helpful to engage in self-exploration and try out different activities and interests. Experimenting with new hobbies or pursuits can help you discover what brings you the most joy and fulfillment.

Overall, having passion is an important aspect of a fulfilling and satisfying life, and can provide a sense of purpose, motivation, and well-being.

GUYS OVER 50
SHOULD BE FLIRTY.

Flirting is a complex social behavior that involves communicating attraction and interest in a potential romantic partner through verbal and nonverbal cues. While some people may view flirting as a harmless and fun way to connect with others, others may view it as inappropriate or uncomfortable.

When it comes to guys over 50, it's important to keep in mind that social norms and expectations around flirting may vary depending on the context and the individual. Some people may view flirting as inappropriate or unwanted, while others may be receptive to it.

It's important to always respect the boundaries and comfort levels of others, and to avoid engaging in behavior that could be perceived as inappropriate or harassing. When flirting, it's important to communicate clearly and respectfully, and to be aware of nonverbal cues and social cues that may indicate discomfort or disinterest.

In general, being friendly and approachable can help you connect with others and potentially find romantic partners. However, it's important to approach flirting with sensitivity and respect, and to be aware of the individual preferences and boundaries of those around you.

GUYS OVER 50 SHOULD HAVE THE QUALITY OF AUTONOMY.

I agree that having the quality of autonomy is important for guys over 50 (and people of all ages) to lead a fulfilling and satisfying life. Autonomy refers to the ability to make decisions and take actions independently, without being overly influenced or controlled by others.

Having a sense of autonomy can be beneficial in many ways. It can help you feel more in control of your life, and can lead to increased confidence and self-esteem. Autonomy can also help you make decisions that align with your values and priorities, and can lead to greater satisfaction and fulfillment.

At the same time, it's important to balance autonomy with collaboration and connection with others. Being overly independent or self-reliant can lead to feelings of isolation and loneliness, which can have negative impacts on mental and physical health.

Finding a healthy balance between autonomy and social connection can help you lead a more fulfilling and satisfying life. This may involve seeking out supportive relationships, engaging in meaningful activities and pursuits, and developing a strong sense of self-worth and identity.

Overall, the quality of autonomy can be an important aspect of a fulfilling and satisfying life, and can help you make decisions and take actions that align with your values and priorities.

GUYS OVER 50
SHOULD SET BOUNDARIES.

I agree that setting boundaries is an important aspect of healthy relationships and self-care for guys over 50 (and people of all ages). Boundaries refer to limits that you set for yourself in order to protect your physical, emotional, and mental well-being, and to ensure that your needs and values are respected.

Setting boundaries can help you maintain healthy relationships, as it can prevent others from crossing lines that you are uncomfortable with, and can help you communicate your needs and expectations clearly. It can also help you avoid being taken advantage of or mistreated, and can help you prioritize your own needs and goals.

However, setting boundaries can be challenging, especially if you are not used to asserting your needs or saying no to others. It's important to remember that setting boundaries is a healthy and necessary aspect of self-care, and that it is okay to prioritize your own well-being and needs.

When setting boundaries, it's important to communicate them clearly and respectfully to others. This may involve saying no to requests or behaviors that are not aligned with your values or needs, or communicating your expectations for how you want to be treated in a relationship.

In summary, setting boundaries is an important aspect of healthy relationships and self-care for guys over 50 (and people of all ages). It can help you protect your well-being, communicate your needs and expectations clearly, and prioritize your own goals and values.

GUYS OVER 50 SHOULD BE SECURE ENOUGH TO WALK AWAY IF THEY WANT.

I agree that guys over 50 (and people of all ages) should be secure enough to walk away from a situation or relationship if it no longer serves their well-being or aligns with their values and goals. Walking away can be difficult, especially if you have invested time, energy, and emotions into a situation or relationship. However, it's important to prioritize your own well-being and needs, and to make decisions that are in alignment with your values and goals.

Walking away can be a sign of strength and self-respect, as it shows that you are willing to prioritize your own needs and goals over external pressures or expectations. It can also help you avoid being taken advantage of or mistreated, and can help you maintain healthy boundaries and relationships.

It's important to remember that walking away does not mean giving up or being weak. It means acknowledging when a situation or relationship is no longer serving your needs or aligning with your values, and taking steps to prioritize your own well-being and happiness.

In summary, being secure enough to walk away from a situation or relationship is an important aspect of self-care and well-being for guys over 50 (and people of all ages). It can help you maintain healthy boundaries and relationships, prioritize your own needs and goals, and avoid being taken advantage of or mistreated.

GUYS OVER 50 SHOULD HAVE HIGH STANDARDS.

I agree that guys over 50 (and people of all ages) should have high standards for themselves and the people they allow into their lives. Having high standards means setting expectations for how you want to be treated, and what you are willing to accept and tolerate in your relationships and interactions with others.

Having high standards can help you maintain healthy boundaries and relationships, and can prevent you from settling for less than you deserve or compromising your values and priorities. It can also help you prioritize your own well-being and happiness, and avoid being taken advantage of or mistreated.

However, it's important to balance having high standards with being open and flexible in your interactions with others. Being too rigid or inflexible can prevent you from building meaningful connections with others, and can limit your opportunities for growth and learning.

When setting standards, it's important to consider what is most important to you and what aligns with your values and priorities. This may involve setting expectations for how you want to be treated, what behaviors you are willing to accept or tolerate, and what qualities you value in others.

In summary, having high standards can be an important aspect of self-care and well-being for guys over 50 (and people of all ages). It can help you maintain healthy boundaries and relationships, prioritize your own well-being and happiness, and avoid being taken advantage of or mistreated.

GUYS OVER 50 SHOULD SEE THEMSELVES AS HIGH VALUE GUYS.

I agree that guys over 50 (and people of all ages) should see themselves as high-value individuals who bring unique qualities and experiences to their relationships and interactions with others.

Viewing oneself as high value can help boost self-esteem and confidence, and can promote a positive self-image. It can also help you attract and build relationships with people who value and appreciate your unique qualities and contributions.

To view oneself as high value, it's important to recognize and appreciate your own strengths, skills, and experiences, and to cultivate a positive self-image. This may involve focusing on your positive qualities and accomplishments, setting goals and taking steps to achieve them, and engaging in activities that bring you joy and fulfillment.

It's also important to avoid comparing yourself to others or measuring your worth based on external factors such as wealth, status, or physical appearance. Instead, focus on your own values, priorities, and goals, and recognize that your unique qualities and experiences make you a valuable and worthwhile individual.

In summary, viewing oneself as a high-value individual can promote self-esteem, confidence, and positive self-image for guys over 50 (and people of all ages). It can also help attract and build relationships with people who appreciate and value your unique qualities and contributions.

GUYS OVER 50
SHOULD HAVE STRONG OPINIONS.

I believe that guys over 50 (and people of all ages) should have the ability to form and express strong opinions on various topics. Having strong opinions can be an important aspect of individuality and can help individuals communicate their values, beliefs, and perspectives to others.

Expressing strong opinions can also be beneficial in fostering healthy relationships, as it can help people connect with others who share similar views and beliefs, and can facilitate open and honest communication. Additionally, having strong opinions can help individuals advocate for themselves and others, and can empower them to take action towards achieving their goals and priorities.

However, it's important to recognize that expressing strong opinions also requires a degree of respect and openness towards differing viewpoints. While it's important to communicate one's beliefs and values, it's equally important to listen to and consider the perspectives of others, and to engage in respectful and constructive dialogue.

In summary, having strong opinions can be an important aspect of individuality and can facilitate healthy relationships and communication for guys over 50 (and people of all ages). However, it's also important to balance this with respect and openness towards differing viewpoints, in order to foster a culture of constructive dialogue and mutual understanding.

GUYS OVER 50 SHOULD NOT BE AGREEABLE WITH EVERYTHING.

I agree that guys over 50 (and people of all ages) should not be agreeable with everything. While it's important to be respectful and open-minded towards others, it's also important to have the ability to form and express one's own opinions and beliefs, even if they differ from others.

Being overly agreeable can lead to a lack of assertiveness and can make it difficult to communicate one's needs and desires effectively. It can also lead to a lack of personal growth and development, as individuals may be hesitant to challenge themselves or try new things if it means going against the status quo or the opinions of others.

However, it's important to recognize that disagreeing with others should be done in a respectful and constructive manner, and that it's possible to express differing opinions without being confrontational or dismissive. It's also important to listen to and consider the perspectives of others, even if they differ from your own, in order to foster a culture of constructive dialogue and mutual understanding.

In summary, while it's important to be respectful and open-minded towards others, guys over 50 (and people of all ages) should have the ability to form and express their own opinions and beliefs, even if they differ from others. Disagreeing with others should be done in a respectful and constructive manner, and it's important to listen to and consider the perspectives of others in order to foster a culture of mutual understanding and growth.

GUYS OVER 50
SHOULD BE FUN.

I believe that guys over 50 (and people of all ages) should strive to have fun and enjoy life. Having a sense of fun can help individuals maintain a positive outlook on life, reduce stress, and improve overall well-being.

Being fun can mean different things to different people, but it can include activities such as trying new things, being adventurous, having a sense of humor, and being social. Engaging in these activities can help individuals stay active and engaged, and can help them build new connections and relationships.

Being fun can also be an important aspect of healthy relationships, as it can help individuals connect with others on a more personal level and can help foster a sense of shared experiences and memories.

In summary, being fun can be an important aspect of overall well-being and can help individuals stay active and engaged, build new connections and relationships, and maintain a positive outlook on life. Guys over 50 (and people of all ages) should strive to incorporate fun activities and experiences into their lives, and prioritize enjoying life to the fullest.

GUYS OVER 50
SHOULD HAVE THEIR ACT
TOGETHER.

I believe that guys over 50 (and people of all ages) should strive to have their act together, or in other words, have their life in order. This can mean different things to different people, but it generally involves having a level of stability, responsibility, and self-awareness in various aspects of one's life.

Having one's act together can include things like having a stable job or source of income, being financially responsible and having a plan for retirement, maintaining good physical and mental health, having a strong support network of friends and family, and being aware of one's personal values and goals.

Striving to have one's act together can help individuals feel more confident and secure in their lives, and can help them navigate challenges and setbacks more effectively. It can also be an important aspect of maintaining healthy relationships, as it can help individuals be more reliable and supportive partners, friends, and family members.

In summary, striving to have one's act together can be an important aspect of overall well-being and can help individuals feel more confident, secure, and prepared for the future. Guys over 50 (and people of all ages) should prioritize stability, responsibility, and self-awareness in various aspects of their lives, and work towards achieving their personal goals and values.

GUYS OVER 50 SHOULD PROJECT THEMSELVES AS A PRIZE.

I believe that guys over 50 (and people of all ages) should strive to project themselves as a prize. This means having a confident and self-assured demeanor, and valuing oneself as a valuable and desirable individual.

Projecting oneself as a prize can involve various aspects of one's life, such as maintaining good physical and mental health, having a fulfilling and purposeful career, pursuing hobbies and interests, and being confident in one's personal values and beliefs. It can also involve being respectful and considerate of others, while still maintaining healthy boundaries and being true to oneself.

When individuals project themselves as a prize, they are more likely to attract others who share similar values and outlooks on life. It can also help them feel more confident and fulfilled in their personal and professional lives, and can help them navigate challenges and setbacks with greater ease.

In summary, projecting oneself as a prize can be an important aspect of overall well-being and can help individuals feel more confident, self-assured, and fulfilled. Guys over 50 (and people of all ages) should strive to value themselves as valuable and desirable individuals, and project a confident and self-assured demeanor in their personal and professional lives.

GUYS OVER 50
SHOULD NOT PUT WOMEN ON A
PEDESTAL.

I believe that guys over 50 (and people of all ages) should avoid putting women on a pedestal. While it's natural to feel attraction and admiration towards someone, placing someone on a pedestal can lead to unrealistic expectations and potential disappointment.

Putting women on a pedestal can involve idealizing them or placing them on a higher level of importance than oneself, which can lead to feelings of inadequacy or insecurity. This can also lead to putting the woman's needs and desires before one's own, which can be detrimental to one's personal growth and well-being.

Instead of putting women on a pedestal, it's important for guys over 50 to see women as individuals with their own strengths, weaknesses, and unique personalities. This can involve developing an authentic and equal relationship with them, based on mutual respect and shared values.

In summary, guys over 50 (and people of all ages) should strive to avoid putting women on a pedestal and instead see them as equal individuals with their own unique qualities and perspectives. This can help foster healthy and authentic relationships based on mutual respect and shared values.

THE DATING GAME

When it comes to dating, I find these 4 things guys get wrong:

They are needy.

They have low value of yourself.

They dress like crap.

They smell bad.

Dating should be a part of your life, but not your entire life. Women should complement your life, not be the focus of your life. But remember, it's never too late to date. That's right! It's never too late to start dating or to find love. Whether you're in your 50s, 60s, 70s, or beyond, there are still plenty of opportunities to meet new people and connect with others who share your interests and values. It's important to remember that dating at any age can come with its own unique challenges, but with the right mindset and approach, it's possible to find fulfilling and meaningful relationships no matter what your age.

GUYS OVER 50 NEED TO PUT THEMSELVES OUT THERE.

This can mean taking steps to expand your social circle, such as joining clubs or groups that align with your interests, or attending social events and gatherings. It can also mean using online dating platforms or apps to connect with potential partners.

Putting yourself out there can feel intimidating or uncomfortable, but it's important to remember that taking risks and stepping out of your comfort zone can lead to new opportunities and experiences. By being open to new possibilities and actively seeking out connections with others, you increase your chances of finding a compatible partner and building fulfilling relationships.

It's also important to be patient and persistent in your efforts to put yourself out there. Building meaningful connections takes time and effort, and it's important to approach the process with a positive and optimistic mindset. By staying true to yourself and your values, and being open to new experiences and perspectives, you can create a fulfilling and rewarding dating and social life.

GUYS OVER 50
SHOULD BE ON A DATING APP.

Dating apps allow you to easily connect with other singles who share similar interests and preferences, and can provide a convenient way to communicate and get to know someone before deciding to meet in person. They also offer a wider pool of potential partners than you may encounter in your daily life.

While dating apps can be a useful tool, it's important to approach them with a healthy mindset and to prioritize safety. This means being honest about your intentions and expectations, and being respectful and considerate in your interactions with others.

It's also important to take steps to protect your privacy and safety when using dating apps, such as being cautious about sharing personal information and meeting in public places for the first few dates.

Ultimately, whether or not to use a dating app is a personal decision that depends on your individual preferences and comfort level. If you're interested in meeting new people and potentially finding a romantic partner, a dating app can be a useful tool to consider.

HOW DO GUYS OVER 50 MAKE THEMSELVES INTO THE PERFECT DATE.

Here are some tips for guys over 50 to make themselves into the perfect date:

1. Be punctual: Arrive on time for your date. This shows that you respect your date's time and that you are reliable.

2. Dress well: Take the time to dress nicely for your date. Make sure your outfit is clean, pressed, and fits well.

3. Be a good listener: Show interest in what your date has to say. Listen actively and respond thoughtfully.

4. Be confident: Confidence is attractive. Don't be afraid to share your opinions or be yourself.

5. Be respectful: Treat your date with respect and kindness. Open doors, pull out chairs, and be polite.

6. Have a positive attitude: A positive attitude is contagious. Be upbeat and optimistic.

7. Be engaging: Ask your date questions about their interests and hobbies. Share your own stories and experiences.

8. Be thoughtful: small gestures like bringing flowers or remembering your date's favorite restaurant can go a long way.

9. Be honest: Be truthful about yourself and your intentions. Don't try to be someone you're not.

10. Be fun: Dates are meant to be enjoyable. Don't take things too seriously and be willing to have a good time.

GUYS OVER 50

SHOULD BE ATTRACTIVE TO ATTRACT PRETTY WOMEN.

Attractiveness is subjective and can vary from person to person. However, there are certain things that can make a man over 50 more attractive to others:

1. Good hygiene: It's important to take care of personal hygiene, such as showering regularly, brushing teeth, and wearing clean clothes.

2. Physical fitness: Regular exercise and a healthy diet can help men over 50 maintain a fit and attractive appearance.

3. Positive attitude: A positive attitude can make a man more attractive and appealing to others.

4. Sense of humor: A good sense of humor can help ease tension and make the date more enjoyable.

5. Confidence: Being confident in oneself can make a man more attractive and appealing to others.

6. Good conversational skills: Having good conversational skills can help keep the conversation flowing and make the date

more engaging.

7. Emotional maturity: Emotional maturity can be attractive to women, as it shows that the man is able to handle situations with grace and maturity.

GUYS OVER 50 SHOULD LEARN FROM THEIR DATING EXPERIENCES.

Yes, learning from experiences is a valuable trait for anyone, including guys over 50. Life is full of ups and downs, and every experience we have is an opportunity to learn and grow. By reflecting on their experiences, guys over 50 can gain insights and wisdom that can help them navigate future challenges and make better decisions. It's important to be open to learning and not repeat the same mistakes, but also to recognize and appreciate the good things that have happened in their lives.

Dating can be a valuable learning experience for men over 50, as it can help them discover more about themselves, their desires, and their preferences. Here are a few ways that men over 50 can learn from their dating experiences:

1. Reflect on past relationships: Men over 50 can reflect on their past relationships to identify patterns or behaviors that may have contributed to the relationship's success or failure. This can help them identify areas for growth or improvement in future relationships.

2. Be open to new experiences: Men over 50 can also approach dating with an open mind and heart, being willing to try new things and meet new people. This can help them expand their horizons and discover new aspects of themselves and their preferences.

3. Practice communication skills: Effective communication is key to any successful relationship, and men over 50 can use their dating experiences to practice and improve their communication skills. This can include active listening, expressing needs and desires, and setting boundaries.

4. Be honest with oneself and others: Honesty and authenticity are important in any relationship, and men over 50 can use their dating experiences to practice being honest with themselves and others. This can involve being clear about what they want and need in a relationship, as well as being upfront about any dealbreakers or non-negotiables.

5. Take time to reflect and learn: Finally, men over 50 can take time to reflect on their dating experiences and learn from them. This can involve journaling, talking with trusted friends or a therapist, or simply taking time to process emotions and thoughts about the dating experience.

In summary, men over 50 can learn a great deal from their dating experiences by reflecting on past relationships, being open to new experiences, practicing communication skills, being honest with themselves and others, and taking time to reflect and learn. By learning from their dating experiences, men over 50 can approach future relationships with greater self-awareness and confidence.

GUYS OVER 50 SHOULD COMMUNICATE VERY WELL ON DATES.

Effective communication is important on dates for guys over 50. Here are a few tips to improve communication:

1. Listen attentively: Focus on the conversation and show your interest by actively listening to your date.

2. Ask open-ended questions: Ask questions that encourage your date to share more about themselves and their interests.

3. Avoid interrupting: Let your date finish their thoughts before adding your own input to the conversation.

4. Share your own experiences: Don't be afraid to share your own experiences and opinions in the conversation. This can help to create a deeper connection.

5. Be respectful and polite: Treat your date with respect and politeness, even if you disagree with them on certain topics.

Remember, communication is a two-way street, so it's important to both listen and contribute to the conversation.

GUYS OVER 50 SHOULD HAVE FUN ON DATES.

Absolutely! Dating should be an enjoyable experience for people of all ages, including men over 50. Here are a few ways that men over 50 can have fun on dates:

1. Plan interesting activities: Men over 50 can plan dates that involve interesting activities, such as trying a new restaurant, attending a concert or cultural event, or going for a hike or bike ride. This can help add a sense of excitement and novelty to the date.

2. Focus on the present moment: Sometimes, men over 50 can get caught up in worries about the future or regrets about the past. To have fun on a date, it can be helpful to focus on the present moment and enjoy the company of the other person.

3. Be open and curious: Men over 50 can approach dates with a sense of openness and curiosity, being willing to learn more about the other person's interests, values, and perspectives. This can help them discover new things and have interesting conversations.

4. Don't take things too seriously: Dating can sometimes feel high-pressure or stressful, but men over 50 can have fun by not taking things too seriously. Laughing and having a sense of humor can help make the date more enjoyable for everyone involved.

5. Be yourself: Finally, the most important way for men over 50 to have fun on dates is to be themselves. Authenticity and vulnerability can help create a deeper connection with the other person and make the date more enjoyable overall.

In summary, men over 50 can have fun on dates by planning interesting activities, focusing on the present moment, being open and curious, not taking things too seriously, and being themselves. By approaching dates with a sense of openness, curiosity, and authenticity, men over 50 can have enjoyable and fulfilling dating experiences.

GUYS OVER 50 SHOULD DATE WOMEN CLOSE TO THEIR AGE.

While there is no one-size-fits-all answer to this question, dating women close to your age can have a number of advantages. For one, it can be easier to find common ground and shared experiences with someone who is in a similar stage of life. Additionally, dating someone who is closer to your age may help to reduce some of the power imbalances or expectations that can come with dating someone much younger.

Of course, age should not be the only factor in determining who you choose to date or form a relationship with. It's important to consider factors like shared values, interests, and personality traits, as well as the ability to communicate and connect on a deeper level.

Ultimately, the most important thing is to choose a partner who you feel comfortable and happy with, and who shares your goals and values for the future. Whether that means dating someone close to your age or someone younger or older, the key is to be true to yourself and to prioritize what is most important to you in a relationship.

GUYS OVER 50
TEND TO GET INTERVIEWED WHILE ON A DATE.

It's possible that some women may ask guys over 50 questions during a date that could feel like an interview. This may happen if the woman is genuinely interested in getting to know the man and is trying to find common ground and establish a connection. However, if it feels like a job interview and is uncomfortable, the man can try redirecting the conversation to more light-hearted or fun topics, or gently communicate his feelings to the woman.

Ultimately, both parties should strive for a balanced conversation where both people feel comfortable and engaged.

GUYS OVER 50 SHOULD PAY ATTENTION TO THEIR DATES.

Paying attention to your date is important at any age, but it can be especially important for guys over 50 who may be more experienced in dating and may have developed certain habits or routines. Here are some tips on how guys over 50 can pay attention to their dates:

1. Listen actively: When your date is talking, make sure to listen actively and show that you are engaged in the conversation. This means making eye contact, nodding your head, and responding appropriately.

2. Ask questions: Asking questions about your date's interests, hobbies, and experiences shows that you are interested in getting to know them better.

3. Be present: Put away your phone and other distractions and focus on the person in front of you. Being present and engaged can make a big difference in how your date perceives you.

4. Show appreciation: If your date does something nice for you, make sure to show your appreciation. A simple "thank you" or compliment can go a long way in building a connection.

5. Respect boundaries: Pay attention to your date's boundaries and make sure to respect them. This includes physical boundaries, but also emotional boundaries like how much personal information they are comfortable sharing.

GUYS OVER 50

SHOULD DATE LIKE A TEEN, BUT AS AN ADULT.

While it's important to maintain a sense of fun and playfulness in dating, it's also important for guys over 50 to approach dating with maturity and perspective. Here are some tips for dating like an adult while still having fun:

1. Be honest and upfront about your intentions: If you're looking for a serious relationship, make that clear from the start. If you're just looking for a casual fling, be honest about that too.

2. Respect your date: Treat your date with respect and kindness, just as you would like to be treated. Listen to what they have to say and show genuine interest in their thoughts and feelings.

3. Take the lead: While it's important to be flexible and accommodating, it's also important to take the lead and plan the date. This shows that you are confident and decisive.

4. Embrace your age: Don't try to act like a teenager or pretend that you're younger than you are. Embrace your age and experience, and use it to your advantage.

5. Have fun: Dating should be fun and enjoyable, so don't take things too seriously. Laugh, smile, and enjoy the moment.

GUYS OVER 50
SHOULD NOT BE SEXTING
YOUNGER WOMEN.

It is generally not appropriate for guys over 50 to engage in sexting with younger women. Not only can this behavior be seen as predatory and inappropriate, but it may also be illegal, depending on the age of the individuals involved.

Moreover, engaging in sexual conversations and activities with younger women can create power imbalances and may not be consensual, which can be harmful to the younger woman's well-being.

Instead, guys over 50 should seek relationships with women who are of a similar age and life experience. It's important to build relationships on mutual respect and consent, and to ensure that both parties are comfortable with any sexual conversations or activities.

If a guy over 50 is struggling with sexual impulses or urges that he feels are inappropriate or harmful, it may be helpful to seek the support of a therapist or counselor. They can help him develop healthy coping strategies and work through any underlying issues that may be contributing to these impulses.

GUYS OVER 50 SHOULD NOT SPEND ALL THEIR SAVINGS TRYING TO IMPRESS A GIRL.

It's important for men over 50 (or anyone, for that matter) to be responsible with their finances and not spend all their savings trying to impress someone they are dating. While it's natural to want to make a good impression and show someone that you care, it's important to do so within the limits of what you can comfortably afford.

Here are some tips to help men over 50 navigate the financial aspects of dating:

1. Set a budget: Before going on dates, it can be helpful to set a budget for how much you want to spend. This can help you avoid overspending and ensure that you are being responsible with your finances.

2. Be honest: If you are not comfortable with a particular activity or expense, it's important to be honest with your date about it. You can suggest alternative activities or simply explain that you need to be mindful of your finances.

3. Focus on quality time: It's not always necessary to spend a lot of money to have a great date. Focus on quality time spent together, such as going for a walk or having a picnic in the park.

4. Consider alternative dates: Instead of always going out for dinner and drinks, consider alternative and more budget-friendly date ideas, such as attending a free event or trying a new activity together.

5. Don't try to impress with material things: Remember that true connection and attraction is not based on material possessions or lavish spending. Focus on being yourself and building a connection with your date based on shared interests and values.

In summary, it's important for men over 50 to be responsible with their finances and not spend all their savings trying to impress someone they are dating. By setting a budget, being honest, focusing on quality time, considering alternative dates, and not trying to impress with material things, men over 50 can have fulfilling and enjoyable dating experiences without breaking the bank.

GUYS OVER 50 SHOULD BE OPEN TO DATING OTHER RACES.

It's important for people of all ages to be open to dating people of different races and ethnicities. Dating someone from a different race can be a valuable and enriching experience, as it allows you to learn about different cultures and perspectives.

Here are some reasons why men over 50 should be open to dating other races:

1. Diversity: Dating someone from a different race can broaden your horizons and expose you to different ways of life and thinking.

2. Growth: Dating someone from a different race can challenge your assumptions and biases, and help you grow as a person.

3. Compatibility: It's important to focus on compatibility with someone, rather than their race or ethnicity. By being open to dating other races, you may find that you have more in common with someone than you initially thought.

4. Breaking down barriers: By dating someone from a different race, you can help break down cultural barriers and promote understanding and acceptance.

It's important to approach dating with an open mind and heart, and to be respectful of different cultures and backgrounds. By being open to dating other races, men over 50 can have meaningful and rewarding relationships with people from all walks of life.

GUYS OVER 50
SHOULD NOT SEND DICK PICS.

Yes, sending unsolicited sexual images or messages, including "dick pics," is inappropriate behavior regardless of one's age or gender. It can be perceived as disrespectful, intrusive, and even harassment. In addition to potentially causing discomfort or distress to the recipient, sending sexually explicit images or messages can also have legal consequences. In many jurisdictions, it can be considered a form of harassment, and may result in criminal charges or civil lawsuits. It's important for older guys to respect boundaries and to communicate with potential partners in a respectful and appropriate manner. This means obtaining clear consent before engaging in any sexual activity, and avoiding any behavior that could be interpreted as harassing or intrusive. By respecting others and practicing responsible communication, older guys can cultivate positive relationships and avoid any unnecessary legal or social complications.

Guys over 50 should not send inappropriate pics of themself.

Yes, sending inappropriate or unsolicited images of oneself can be inappropriate and potentially harmful behavior. This is true regardless of age or gender.

Sending inappropriate pictures of oneself can be seen as intrusive, disrespectful, and even harassing. It can also cause discomfort or distress to the recipient and may even lead to legal consequences.

In addition to being inappropriate, sending such images can also damage one's reputation and make it difficult to establish positive relationships with others.

It's important for guys over 50 to respect boundaries and communicate with potential partners in a respectful and appropriate manner. This includes avoiding any behavior that could be interpreted as harassing or intrusive, and obtaining clear consent before engaging in any sexual activity.

By practicing responsible communication and respecting others' boundaries, guys over 50 can build positive relationships and avoid any unnecessary legal or social complications.

GUYS OVER 50

SHOULD NOT PROJECT THEIR FEELINGS ON THEIR DATES.

It's important for anyone, regardless of age or gender, to avoid projecting their feelings onto their dates. When someone projects their feelings, they are essentially attributing their own thoughts and emotions onto their date, without considering that the other person may have a different perspective or experience.

Here are a few reasons why guys over 50 should avoid projecting their feelings onto their dates:

1. Miscommunication: If you're projecting your feelings onto your date, you may not be communicating clearly and effectively. This can lead to misunderstandings and misinterpretations, which can cause unnecessary conflict and tension.

2. Lack of empathy: Projecting your feelings onto your date can prevent you from being empathetic and understanding of their thoughts and emotions. This can make it difficult to build a genuine connection and rapport.

3. Unhealthy boundaries: When you project your feelings onto your date, you may be crossing boundaries that aren't healthy or appropriate. This can make your date feel uncomfortable or overwhelmed, which can damage the relationship.

Instead of projecting your feelings onto your date, it's important to listen actively, be present in the moment, and try to understand their perspective. It's also important to be honest and open about your own feelings, without assuming that your date feels the same way. By communicating clearly and respecting each other's boundaries, you can build a healthy and fulfilling relationship.

GUYS OVER 50
SHOULD LEARN FROM EACH DATE THEY GO ON.

Dating can be a valuable learning experience, regardless of whether or not the date leads to a long-term relationship. Each date can provide an opportunity to learn more about yourself and what you're looking for in a partner, as well as to gain insight into different perspectives and experiences.

To make the most of each date, it's important to approach it with an open mind and a willingness to listen and learn. This means asking questions, actively listening to your date's responses, and being open to new ideas and perspectives.

It's also important to reflect on each date afterwards, thinking about what went well and what could have been improved. By learning from each date, you can better understand your own needs and preferences, and increase your chances of finding a compatible partner in the future.

THE PROS AND CONS OF
DATING YOUNGER WOMEN.

It's important to keep in mind that relationships with large age gaps can come with unique challenges. These challenges may include differences in life experience, interests, and goals, as well as potential social stigmas and judgment from others.

Additionally, it's important to ensure that any relationship is built on mutual respect, trust, and consent. If one partner is significantly older than the other, it's important to ensure that the power dynamic in the relationship is healthy and balanced.

Ultimately, when it comes to dating, it's important to prioritize compatibility and respect for one another, regardless of age. Each person should make their own decisions about who they want to date based on their individual values and preferences.

Dating younger women can have both advantages and disadvantages, and it's important to consider both before pursuing a relationship with someone who is significantly younger than you.

Pros:

1. Physical attraction: Many men find younger women to be physically attractive, and the vitality and energy that comes

with youth can be an appealing factor.

2. Shared interests: If you're dating someone younger, you may find that you have shared interests and hobbies that you can enjoy together.

3. Positive outlook: Younger women often have a more positive outlook on life, and can bring a fresh perspective and enthusiasm to a relationship.

4. Learning opportunities: Dating someone younger can provide opportunities for personal growth and learning, as you may be exposed to new ideas, experiences, and ways of thinking.

Cons:

1. Different life stages: If you're dating someone significantly younger, you may be at different stages in your lives, which can create challenges in terms of long-term compatibility.

2. Generational differences: There may be significant differences in cultural references, values, and communication styles between someone from a different generation, which can make it harder to relate to each other.

3. Power imbalances: In some cases, an age gap can create a power imbalance in a relationship, particularly if the older partner has significantly more life experience or financial resources.

4. Social stigma: Some people may judge or disapprove of a relationship with a significant age gap, which can create social tension and cause stress for both partners.

Ultimately, whether dating a younger woman is a good choice for you depends on your individual preferences and circumstances. It's important to approach any relationship with honesty, respect, and open communication, and to consider the potential challenges and benefits before making a decision.

DATING SOMEONE WITH A LARGE AGE GAP CAN COME WITH UNIQUE CHALLENGES.

Here are some potential cons to consider:

1. Differences in life experience: Depending on the age gap, there may be significant differences in life experience between partners. This can lead to differences in interests, goals, and perspectives that may create challenges in the relationship.

2. Societal judgment: Relationships with large age gaps may face judgment or stigma from society. This can create added pressure and stress for both partners, and may affect the way others perceive and treat the couple.

3. Health concerns: Depending on the age gap, there may be differences in health and physical ability between partners. This can create challenges in terms of activity level and lifestyle compatibility.

4. Power dynamics: Relationships with large age gaps may create power imbalances, particularly if one partner is significantly

older than the other. This can create challenges in terms of decision-making, communication, and the overall health of the relationship.

5. Family and social circle differences: Depending on the age gap, there may be differences in family and social circle dynamics between partners. This can create challenges in terms of social integration and compatibility with each other's networks.

It's important to keep in mind that every relationship is unique, and what may be a challenge for one couple may not be for another. Ultimately, the decision to date someone with a large age gap should be made based on individual values and preferences, and should prioritize communication, mutual respect, and consent.

IMMATURE WOMEN ARE MORE LIKELY TO BE FLAKY.

It's possible that someone who is immature may be more likely to be flaky in a relationship. This could be because they struggle with setting and respecting boundaries, or because they have difficulty prioritizing their commitments and responsibilities. Additionally, someone who is immature may struggle with communication, making it more difficult to plan and follow through on plans.

However, it's important to keep in mind that not all immature people are flaky, and not all flaky people are immature. There may be a variety of reasons why someone is unreliable in a relationship, and it's important to assess each situation individually.

If you're dating someone who is consistently flaky, it's important to communicate openly and honestly about how their behavior is affecting you and your relationship. If the person is willing to work on improving their reliability and communication, it may be possible to build a stronger, healthier relationship. However, if the person is unwilling or unable to change their behavior, it may be best to consider ending the relationship in order to prioritize your own needs and well-being.

DATING SOMEONE WHO IS IMMATURE CAN COME WITH A VARIETY OF CHALLENGES.

Here are some potential cons to consider:

1. Lack of emotional maturity: Immaturity often translates to a lack of emotional maturity, which can lead to difficulties in communication, conflict resolution, and overall relationship health.

2. Different priorities: If someone is immature, they may have different priorities than you do. This can create challenges in terms of goal setting, decision-making, and long-term planning.

3. Impulsive behavior: Immature people may be more likely to engage in impulsive or reckless behavior, which can create challenges in terms of trust and safety in the relationship.

4. Difficulty with boundaries: Immature people may struggle with boundaries, both in terms of setting and respecting them. This can create challenges in terms of respecting each other's needs and wants.

5. Incompatibility: Depending on the degree of immaturity, it's possible that you and the other person may simply be incompatible in terms of your personalities, communication styles, and overall values.

Ultimately, the decision to date someone who is immature is a personal one that should be made based on individual values and preferences. It's important to prioritize communication, mutual respect, and setting healthy boundaries in any relationship, regardless of the other person's maturity level. If you find that the challenges of dating someone who is immature outweigh the benefits, it may be best to consider ending the relationship.

A YOUNGER WOMAN
IS MORE LIKELY TO LEAVE AN
OLDER GUY.

It's important to avoid making sweeping generalizations about people based solely on their age or gender. While it's true that a younger woman may be more likely to leave an older man, this is not always the case.

Ultimately, the success of a relationship depends on a variety of factors, including communication, mutual respect, shared values and interests, and emotional compatibility. While age can be a factor in a relationship, it is by no means the only or most important factor.

It's important to prioritize open and honest communication with your partner, regardless of their age or gender. This means being willing to listen to their concerns and needs, as well as expressing your own feelings and desires in a respectful and non-judgmental way. By working together as a team, you can build a strong and healthy relationship that is based on trust, respect, and mutual understanding.

Ultimately, dating someone who has children requires a willingness to be patient, understanding, and flexible. By working together and building a positive relationship with the children, it is possible to create a strong and healthy relationship that can withstand the unique challenges of blended families.

GUYS OVER 50
DATING PROFILES

Here are some tips that may help you create a compelling dating profile if you're over 50:

1. Be honest and authentic: It's essential to be honest about who you are, your interests, and what you're looking for in a relationship. Avoid exaggerating your qualities or hiding your flaws.

2. Use a recent and flattering photo: A clear and current photo of yourself can increase your chances of getting matches. Make sure it's a good quality image that showcases your personality and style.

3. Write an engaging bio: Your bio should highlight your personality, values, and interests. It's also an opportunity to show your sense of humor and talk about what you're looking for in a relationship.

4. Be positive: Avoid negative language and focus on the positive aspects of your life. You want to attract people who are interested in your personality and lifestyle.

5. Keep it simple: Don't overload your profile with too much information. Keep it concise and easy to read. You want to make a good impression without overwhelming potential matches.

6. Be open-minded: Be open to meeting people from different backgrounds and with different interests. You never know who you might connect with!

Remember, your dating profile is your chance to showcase your personality and find someone who shares your values and interests. Take your time and put some effort into creating a profile that represents who you are. Good luck!

GUYS OVER 50
NEED TO BE COOL.

It's important to be confident and comfortable with yourself when dating, regardless of your age. However, there's no need to try to be "cool" or try to conform to a certain stereotype to attract a partner. Being yourself and showing your authentic personality is more important than trying to fit a certain mold.

In fact, many people find confidence and self-assuredness attractive, so focus on being confident in who you are and what you bring to the table. It's also important to be respectful, kind, and considerate in your interactions with others, as these qualities can go a long way in building a connection.

Ultimately, the most important thing is to be true to yourself and to show up as the best version of yourself. This will help you attract people who appreciate you for who you are and who you can build a meaningful connection with.

GUYS OVER 50
SHOULD NOT CHASE WOMEN.

It's important to approach dating with respect and consideration for others, regardless of your age. Chasing women can come across as aggressive and may make them feel uncomfortable or pressured. Instead, it's better to show genuine interest and let things unfold naturally.

This doesn't mean you shouldn't take initiative or make the first move. It's perfectly fine to initiate a conversation or ask someone out on a date. However, it's important to be respectful and considerate in your approach, and to take the other person's feelings into consideration.

Remember that dating is a two-way street, and it's important to be mindful of the other person's feelings and boundaries. It's also important to be patient and take things at a pace that's comfortable for both parties. This will help build a connection that's based on mutual respect and understanding, rather than chasing or pressure.

GUYS OVER 50
DON'T NEED TO BE FAKE.

Being fake is never a good idea when it comes to dating, regardless of your age. In fact, as you get older, it becomes even more important to be true to yourself and your values.

Trying to be someone you're not or pretending to have interests that you don't actually have can backfire in the long run. It's better to be authentic and show your true personality, even if it means revealing your flaws or vulnerabilities.

When you're honest and genuine in your interactions with others, you're more likely to attract people who appreciate you for who you are. You'll also have more meaningful and fulfilling relationships with people who share your values and interests.

So, if you're over 50 and looking to date, be yourself and show your true personality. Don't be afraid to reveal your flaws or quirks, as these are often the things that make you unique and interesting to others.

GUYS OVER 50
DON'T BEG WOMEN
TO DATE THEM.

It's important to approach dating with respect and consideration for others, regardless of your age. Begging someone to date you is not a healthy or respectful way to initiate a relationship, and it can make the other person feel uncomfortable or pressured.

Instead of begging, focus on building a connection with someone through mutual interests and respectful communication. Show genuine interest in the other person, ask questions, and listen to their responses. Be patient and take things at a pace that's comfortable for both parties.

Remember that dating is a two-way street, and both parties should feel comfortable and respected throughout the process. If someone isn't interested in dating you, it's important to respect their decision and move on. There are plenty of other people out there who may be a better match for you, so don't get discouraged if things don't work out with one person.

GUYS OVER 50
NEED TO GROW UP.

It's important to approach dating with maturity and responsibility, regardless of your age. However, growing up doesn't necessarily mean giving up on having fun or being adventurous. It means being responsible and respectful in your interactions with others, and being able to handle the ups and downs of a relationship with grace and dignity.

When you're over 50, you have likely experienced a lot of life and have gained valuable insights and perspectives. It's important to use this wisdom to approach dating with a level head and a positive attitude.

This means being honest and direct in your communication with others, respecting their boundaries, and being willing to compromise and work through challenges together. It also means being responsible for your own actions and emotions, and not placing blame on others.

Ultimately, being mature in your approach to dating will help you build more meaningful and fulfilling relationships with others, and will make you a more attractive partner. So, focus on being responsible, respectful, and positive, while still embracing the fun and adventure that comes with dating.

GUYS OVER 50
SHOULD BE A LEADER.

While it's important to be confident and assertive in your interactions with others, being a "leader" may not be the best approach when it comes to dating. A successful relationship is built on mutual respect and communication, rather than one person taking charge or being dominant.

Instead of trying to be a leader, focus on being a partner who is respectful, communicative, and open-minded. Be willing to listen to the other person's opinions and perspectives, and work together to find common ground and solutions to challenges.

It's also important to be supportive and encouraging of your partner's goals and aspirations, and to help them achieve their dreams. This requires empathy, understanding, and a willingness to put the other person's needs and wants before your own at times.

Ultimately, being a good partner is about being there for the other person, listening to their needs, and working together to create a relationship that's based on mutual respect and love.

GUYS OVER 50
SHOULD BE STRAIGHT FORWARD.

Being straightforward and honest is an important trait to have in any relationship, regardless of your age. When you're over 50, you've likely learned that beating around the bush or playing games can lead to misunderstandings and hurt feelings.

In dating, being straightforward means expressing your feelings and intentions clearly and respectfully. It means being honest about your expectations for the relationship and being willing to have open and honest communication with your partner.

Being straightforward also means being able to handle difficult conversations with grace and maturity. This means being able to express your feelings and opinions in a calm and respectful manner, while also being open to listening to the other person's perspective.

When you're straightforward and honest in your approach to dating, you'll build trust and respect with your partner. You'll also be more likely to attract people who appreciate your directness and honesty, and who are looking for the same level of transparency in a relationship.

GUYS OVER 50
DON'T NEED TO SAVE A WOMEN.

It's important to approach relationships as equals, rather than one person feeling like they need to "save" the other. Both partners should be able to support and uplift each other, while also being able to take care of themselves.

The idea of "saving" someone can create an unhealthy power dynamic in a relationship, where one person may feel like they have more control or influence over the other. It's important to recognize that each person is responsible for their own life and well-being, and that it's not one person's job to fix or rescue the other.

Instead of trying to save someone, focus on building a relationship based on mutual respect, support, and encouragement. Be willing to listen to the other person's needs and concerns, and offer your support in a way that is respectful and non-judgmental.

Ultimately, a healthy and successful relationship is built on a foundation of mutual respect, trust, and communication. Both partners should feel like they are able to be themselves and pursue their own goals and interests, while also feeling supported and loved by their partner.

GUYS OVER 50
SHOULD BE "HIGH VALUE".

The idea of being "high value" can be subjective and vary depending on individual preferences and values. However, in general, being a "high value" partner means that you bring positive qualities and attributes to a relationship that are attractive and desirable to your partner.

Some traits that could be considered "high value" in a partner include:

- Honesty and integrity: Being truthful and trustworthy is essential for building a strong foundation of trust in a relationship.

- Emotional intelligence: Being able to communicate effectively, listen actively, and respond empathetically to your partner's emotions can help create a deeper connection and understanding in the relationship.

- Respectful and considerate behavior: Treating your partner with kindness, respect, and consideration is key to building a healthy and loving relationship.

- Personal growth and development: Being committed to your own personal growth and development, and supporting your partner's growth as well, can help create a relationship that's dynamic and fulfilling.

- A sense of humor: Being able to laugh and enjoy each other's company is an important part of any relationship.

Financial stability: Being responsible with money and having a stable financial foundation can help reduce stress and conflict in the relationship.

Ultimately, being a "high value" partner means being someone who brings positive qualities and attributes to the relationship, and who is committed to building a strong, loving, and fulfilling partnership with their partner.

WAYS GUYS OVER 50 CAN GET CONFIDENCE.

If you're looking to boost your confidence as a guy over 50, here are some tips that may help:

1. Focus on your strengths: Take a moment to reflect on your positive qualities and achievements. Whether it's your work ethic, your sense of humor, or your ability to connect with others, focusing on your strengths can help boost your confidence.

2. Practice self-care: Taking care of yourself can have a positive impact on your confidence. This can include regular exercise, eating healthy, getting enough sleep, and engaging in activities that you enjoy.

3. Try something new: Challenging yourself to try something new can help you step out of your comfort zone and build confidence in your abilities. Whether it's learning a new skill or taking up a new hobby, trying new things can help you discover new strengths and capabilities.

4. Surround yourself with positive people: Being around people who uplift and encourage you can have a positive impact on

your confidence. Surround yourself with people who support and believe in you, and who help you feel good about yourself.

5. Practice positive self-talk: The way you talk to yourself can have a big impact on your confidence. Practice speaking to yourself in a positive and encouraging way, and avoid negative self-talk or self-criticism.

6. Seek support if needed: If you're struggling with low confidence, consider seeking support from a counselor or therapist who can help you work through your challenges and build your confidence.

Remember, building confidence is a process that takes time and effort. By taking small steps and practicing self-care and positive self-talk, you can gradually build your confidence and feel more empowered in your daily life.

GUYS OVER 50
SHOULD NOT SAY THEY ARE SORRY
IF THEY ASK A WOMAN OUT.

It's important to be respectful and considerate when asking someone out, regardless of age or gender. If you're interested in asking a woman out, it's okay to express your interest and ask if she would be open to going on a date with you. However, it's also important to be mindful of her response and to respect her decision if she's not interested or if she prefers to just be friends.

If she does say no, it's not necessary to apologize. Simply thank her for her time and let her know that you respect her decision. Saying "sorry" can sometimes come across as overly apologetic or even insincere, so it's okay to simply be gracious and respectful in your response.

Remember that rejection is a natural part of dating, and it's not a reflection of your worth or value as a person. Keep an open mind, stay positive, and continue to put yourself out there if you're interested in meeting new people and exploring romantic connections.

GUYS OVER 50 SHOULD PICK OUT THE PLACE TO EAT.

While it's not necessary for guys over 50 to always pick out the place to eat, it can be a thoughtful gesture to take charge and make the decision. However, it's important to also consider your partner's preferences and dietary restrictions when making a decision.

If you're unsure of what your partner likes or if you want to try something new, it can be helpful to ask for suggestions or do some research beforehand. You can also take turns choosing the restaurant or meal, or plan a meal together to ensure that both of your preferences are taken into account.

Remember that communication is key in any relationship, and it's important to have open and honest discussions about what you both enjoy and prefer when it comes to dining out. Ultimately, the goal should be to find a solution that works for both of you and allows you to enjoy each other's company while sharing a meal.

GUYS OVER 50

SHOULD NOT SAY THEY ARE SORRY FOR TALKING TO A WOMEN IN THEIR DM.

If a guy over 50 reaches out to a woman in her DMs, it's important to be respectful and considerate in their approach. While it's not necessary to apologize for reaching out, it's important to be mindful of the woman's boundaries and comfort level.

If the woman doesn't respond or expresses that she's not interested in continuing the conversation, it's important to respect her decision and not push the issue. In this situation, it's not necessary to apologize, but rather to thank her for her time and let her know that you understand and respect her decision.

If the woman is open to continuing the conversation, it's important to continue to be respectful and mindful of her boundaries. It's okay to express your interest, but be sure to listen to her responses and be open to adjusting your approach based on her comfort level.

Remember that communication and respect are key in any interaction, and it's important to approach others in a way that is considerate and respectful of their feelings and boundaries.

THERE IS NO ONE-SIZE-FITS-ALL ANSWER TO THE BEST ADVICE FOR GUYS OVER 50, AS EVERYONE'S SITUATION AND GOALS ARE DIFFERENT. A GOOD SUMMARY THAT WILL HELP YOU.

1. Take care of your health: As you age, it's important to prioritize your physical and mental health. This includes eating a healthy diet, staying active, getting enough sleep, managing stress, and seeing your doctor regularly.

2. Stay engaged and social: Maintaining social connections and staying engaged in your community can help you stay mentally and emotionally healthy. Join clubs or organizations, volunteer, or attend community events.

3. Pursue your passions: Pursuing your passions and interests can provide a sense of fulfillment and purpose. Make time for your hobbies and explore new interests.

4. Learn new things: Lifelong learning can help keep your mind sharp and prevent cognitive decline. Take classes, read books,

or explore new topics online.

5. Embrace change: Life is full of changes, and it's important to embrace them and adapt to new situations. Don't be afraid to try new things or take risks.

6. Seek help when needed: It's okay to ask for help when you need it. Whether it's seeking advice from a friend or professional help for mental health concerns, don't hesitate to reach out.

7. Pursue your interests: Pursuing your interests and hobbies is a great way to keep learning. Whether it's taking up a new sport, learning a new language, or exploring a new topic of interest, doing something you enjoy can make the learning process more enjoyable and rewarding.

8. Read regularly: Reading is an excellent way to learn new information, expand your knowledge, and stimulate your mind. Make a habit of reading regularly, whether it's books, magazines, or online articles.

9. Take courses: Taking courses, either online or in-person, is a great way to learn new skills and expand your knowledge. Look for courses that interest you and align with your goals.

10. Attend seminars and workshops: Attending seminars and workshops is a great way to learn from experts in a particular field and connect with like-minded individuals.

11. Use technology: Technology offers a wealth of resources for learning. Use the internet to research new topics, watch educational videos, and participate in online courses and webinars.

12. Travel: Traveling can expose you to new cultures, languages, and ways of life. Take advantage of opportunities to travel and learn about the world around you.

13. Stay curious: The most important part of learning is staying curious and open-minded. Maintain a thirst for knowledge and never stop asking questions.

14. Remember, learning is a lifelong process. Embrace opportunities to learn and grow.

Remember, everyone's journey is different, and it's important to prioritize what's important to you. Stay true to yourself, enjoy life's moments, and keep moving forward.

BEST OF ALL:

IF IT DOESN'T APPLY, LET IT FLY!

H.Z.